Summer of Fire

SUMMER OF FIRE

JIM CARRIER

Photographs by

JEFF HENRY *and* TED WOOD

Foreword by

ROBERT BARBEE

GIBBS·SMITH
P
PUBLISHER

PEREGRINE SMITH BOOKS

SALT LAKE CITY

First Edition

93 92 91 90 89   5 4 3 2 1

Published by Gibbs Smith, Publisher, P.O. Box 667,
Layton, UT 84041. This is a Peregrine Smith Book

Design by J. Scott Knudsen

Printed and bound by Sung in Printing Co., Ltd.

in Korea

Library of Congress Cataloging-in-Publication Data
Carrier, Jim, 1944-
    Summer of fire / Jim Carrier ; photographs by Jeff
Henry and Ted Wood ; foreword by Robert Barbee.
        p.   cm.
    "Peregrine Smith book."
    ISBN 0-87905-074-8
    1. Forest fires – Yellowstone National Park.
2. Forest fires – Yellowstone National Park – Pictorial
works. I. Henry, Jeff.   II. Wood, Ted, 1962-
III. Title.
SD421.32.Y4C37   1989
634.9'618'0978752 – dc19   88-37669
                                                              CIP

The paper used in this publication meets the
minimum requirements of American National
Standard for Information Sciences – Permanence of
paper for Printed Library Materials, ANSI Z39.48-1984
∞

To my parents, Al and Rebecca Carrier, with love

Foreword

For those of us who experienced the 1988 Yellowstone fires, a hundred images rush to mind: vignettes of things seen or heard, critical decisions we could make in haste and know we might regret at leisure, and an exhausting rush of moods brought on by natural events we could not control. So much was happening at once; the individual memory does not exist that could absorb and retain it all.

In today's world, memory is almost the same as media, and the public memory of the fires will in large part be a creation of the press. The Yellowstone fires were a great lesson in the peculiar challenges facing a free press. Some coverage was very good, some was sensational, and much was inaccurate. We struggled with this all summer, alternately laughing and groaning at the story as it appeared on the nightly news. Yellowstone is such a magic name, and has such powerful associations for Americans, that the fires generated more emotion than inquiry, and more heat than light. Calmness is a rare quality under the best of circumstances, and a reporter (or a ranger) facing 200-foot flames and blinding smoke is not in the best of circumstances. The public gets its information through many filters, but no better process has ever been devised than the one we have; the press's freedom is important precisely because it does allow so many viewpoints to be aired.

Jim Carrier's book portrays many of those viewpoints, including some held by those of us who were directly involved in managing and fighting the fires. We certainly don't agree with all of the others, or even with all of Jim's conclusions, but we support him in his efforts to present different opinions and interpretations, partly because that's the right way to tell the story and partly because we're confident enough in our own positions that we think they stand up quite well by comparison.

Jim's book can barely suggest the complexity of what happened here, and is rightly only a foreshadowing of the dialogues to come regarding the fires. There will never be unanimity of opinion on the fires, their management, or their effects. But eventually, through the process of which this book is a part, the extremes of opinion and the more ridiculous inaccuracies will be identified and perhaps corrected in the public memory. The process of official review and analysis (and the simultaneous process of personal introspection we all may undergo now that we have time for it) has only begun, and it is as complicated and fascinating as are the ecological processes initiated by the fires. With luck, we'll all learn something from it, if not about the fires then about ourselves.

If you bought this book in the park, you already have had a chance to look around. If not, my best advice is that reading is not enough. Come and visit. Yellowstone Park is still here, and the grand attractions we all love are just as grand. The wildlife, the waterfalls, the geysers, the trout streams, and the sense of peace and beauty are all doing fine. If anything, the park is even more of a treat. Because of the fires and their remarkable ecological aftermath, Yellowstone is now, even more than in the past, both a challenge and a balm for the human spirit. See for yourself.

Robert Barbee
Superintendent
Yellowstone National Park
December 1988

Summer of Fire

IT LOOKED, AT FIRST, LIKE A CAMPFIRE.

A thin, blue gray wisp of smoke above the dark green canopy that stretched away from the lookout windows on Mt. Sheridan. From where George Henley stood in the middle of his stone and shingled perch, the smoke was northwest, across the Red Mountains and Lewis Lake, across the road to Yellowstone's south entrance, just beyond the channel of water that drained Shoshone Lake.

Henley, blond and curly-haired, spun the Osborne Firefinder mounted on a column in the middle of the room, bent his tall frame to aim through the raised eyepiece, and sighted along a map of the green park below him. On a blank paper, he jotted some notes. Then he called on his radio.

"Seven hundred fox, this is 721."

"Go ahead 721."

"I have a smoke to report."

In the fire cache at Mammoth Hot Springs on the other side of Yellowstone, Phil Perkins pulled a government form, and as Henley dictated, began filling in the blanks.

Old Faithful, the most popular attraction at Yellowstone National Park, possessed an eerie beauty throughout the Summer of Fire. (©Ted Wood 1988)

"Fire Number"—Perkins glanced at a board on the wall over his desk and wrote "5."

"Name of Fire"—Henley chose Shoshone, for the lake nearby.

"Location"—UTM 526.7 E, 4909.8 N.

"Size of fire"—Spot.

"Probable Cause"—Lightning.

It was 2:58 P.M. on June 23, 1988. Yellowstone's Summer of Fire had begun.

Perkins took a grease pencil, reached high on the wall and wrote "Shoshone" under four other names: Rose, Observation, Crystal and Cougar—the poetry of the park's geography used by lookouts to christen their fires. Rose and Crystal, born in thunderstorms, had gone out in the rains that followed. Observation was a campfire started by a man near an Old Faithful outlook and put out by a ranger. Cougar would sputter out on its own in a week. Yellowstone's fire season was starting very typically.

Perkins wanted a closer look at the Shoshone fire and asked a ranger to hike to it. At 8:00 P.M., five hours after the fire was spotted, the ranger radioed. The fire measured fifty feet long and ten feet wide and was burning in dead lodgepole pine. There was lots of bare dirt around it and flames were burning downhill. The fire was a mile south of Shoshone Lake, and three-fourths of a mile west of the channel.

Perkins called members of the Fire Committee together at park headquarters, Chief Ranger Dan Sholly and fire ecologist Don Despain among them, to brief them on the park's newest fire. They checked the weather, the terrain, the kind of wood around it, and decided to let it burn.

From Mt. Sheridan, Henley glanced at the smoke from time to time and watched for others through the twenty-three windows of the little square lookout. He saw none. Shoshone was his first. Five days earlier a helicopter had dropped him with food and water and radios on the mountaintop to find the lookout door broken in and the place a mess. He had spent most of his time sweeping up rat leavings and bits of books chewed by pikas during Yellowstone's long winter. He also started a journal.

"I gathered more snow today, filling a third garbage can," Henley wrote. "There were no storms today. Just towering cumulous clouds which disappeared by evening."

The snow, he drank and packed around his fresh food. The next day he collected more.

"It was very hot today, 78 degrees," he wrote. "There were baby marmots by the steps. The Shoshone fire produced lots of smoke from 1500 to sundown."

The next afternoon Roy Renkin, a biologist, and Jane Lopez, a member of a helitak crew, hiked in for a look at Shoshone. They carried sleeping bags and food and planned to stay to monitor the fire, standard procedure under Yellowstone's natural fire program. With the precision of a scientist, Renkin made notes for Perkins. The fire had burned three-quarters of an acre in dead and down wood. He counted twenty-four little smokes with two pockets of flame a meter high. The fire was not spreading. The skies were overcast, with little wind.

"I couldn't see any smoke from the Shoshone fire today, so perhaps it is almost out," Henley wrote two days later. He was wrong. On June 30, it was "smoking good."

As tourists began crowding into Yellowstone for the long July Fourth weekend, they largely were unaware of fire in the park. Henley planned to walk down the trail to pick up fresh food. His meat was spoiling in the heat. As he crawled out of his sleeping bag, washed in a basin with his precious water and took weather observations, he noticed another column of smoke, nearly in line with the Shoshone, but a bit closer. The base of the fire was hidden by the Red Mountains that rolled beneath him, so he assumed the smoke was somewhere in them. He called it Red fire, and it went on the fire cache board as number "9."

Tourists seemed to go about their usual business, even with fires burning nearby. (©Ted Wood 1988)

He also noticed, way off in the distance to the north, the undefined haze of a faraway blaze.

Phil Perkins, the gentle, mustached fire cache chief, was grilling hamburgers at his new home in Mammoth. He was cooking for an informal gathering of the fire crew, a close-knit group of men trained to put out fire. But each felt strongly about letting fires burn in Yellowstone. Fire was a natural and historic part of the ecosystem, a force that invigorated aging forests and released the trees' nutrients for new growth. Since 1972, Yellowstone officials had allowed natural, or lightning, fires to burn as part of its natural regulation of the park.

As the smoke curled up from the hamburgers, Perkins noticed the haze, too, drifting from the west. He knew what it was. The Fan fire, which had started two days after the Shoshone, was burning 1,500 acres in the rugged drainages of the Gallatin Mountain Range. The smoke had drifted across U.S. 191

where Smokey the Bear fire danger signs held the word *high*. But a park radio transmitter set up on the highway broadcast this signal: "Don't be alarmed. Please do not report the fire. Turn your headlights on." As Perkins cooked, the smell of charbroiled hamburger mixed with the faint smell of burning wood, and the fire staff talked of the summer to come.

In West Yellowstone, Montana, members of the volunteer fire department again opened the community fireworks stand and let kids and their parents discharge them in the city park. The firemen put on their annual fireworks show on Monday, the Fourth, during a thunderstorm. "Some of the lightning was prettier than the fireworks," said a dispatcher.

In his bird's nest Henley could only marvel at the display. A lightning rod stuck into the storm from the middle of his peaked roof. Thick copper wires ran away in all directions, down both sides of the knife-edge ridge that

An undefined haze
creeps ahead of the fire
like a silent messenger.
(©Ted Wood 1988)

Biologists believed that
natural fires would
rejuvenate winter range
and begin regenerating
aspen, an important tree
to beaver and browsers.
(©Jeff Henry 1988)

Extreme dryness of grasses and timber, as shown in this grazing area, was the major reason the fires of '88 spread so fast and far. (©Jeff Henry 1988)

Weather

ON A COLD DAY IN FEBRUARY 1988, skiers in the backcountry north of Yellowstone National Park built a fire in the snow to warm themselves. When they skied off, the fire burned down through and underneath the snow, charring one-tenth of an acre in the Gallatin National Forest.

That same month, Steve Frye, the park's Northern District ranger, drove through a blizzard to fight another fire near Whitehall, Montana, northwest of Yellowstone. The fire burned 1,600 acres, fanned by 50-mph winds.

It was a bizarre foreboding.

By spring the signs of drought were everywhere in the West. Barges ran aground in the Mississippi. Farmers' crops rose a few inches and shriveled in the dust. And a time bomb was ticking in Yellowstone.

For most of the 1980s precipitation had been below normal in Yellowstone, and the ground and the woods slowly were drying out. So severe was the drying that in midwinter 1988, even with a cover of snow, Yellowstone's ecosystem was in an extreme drought, according to the Palmer Drought Index, published by the U.S. Weather Bureau. Weather stations in western Wyoming showed the driest year since the dust-bowl years of the 1930s. Even after heavy rains in April and May in Yellowstone, the drought was extreme.

Fire danger ratings measured by Yellowstone's weather stations climbed. One computer-generated rating, "energy release component," showed that fires would be difficult to control in June.

Near Dubois, Wyoming, southeast of the park, one fire in June was burning so intensely that a special machine was brought in to measure the moisture in large logs. On June 28, readings ran as low as 9 percent moisture. Kiln-dried wood in lumber yards contains 12 percent moisture.

Inside the park, moisture readings of 16 to 22 percent held until July 10, when they plummeted to the low teens. By July 18, fuel moisture throughout the park was 9 to 16 percent. By then, nine fires had burned 12,000 acres.

A split in the jet stream kept Pacific moisture from reaching the park as it had done every summer for a century. The last substantial rain had fallen on Memorial Day. Creeks and sloughs dried up, the Yellowstone River grew scummy and shallow, though August and early September moisture levels in wood continued to drop.

the lookout sat on. Static electricity drained away on those wires, and he could feel it and hear it. From his safe house, an electric storm was a front-row seat to glory.

The July 4 storm started three more fires in Yellowstone—Miller, Amethyst and Lava—each evaluated, monitored, and allowed to burn. Especially Lava. Burning in sage and grass along Lava Creek near Mammoth, the fire was important to Yellowstone's northern range, home to the park's largest herds of elk and buffalo. Biologists in the park's research office believed fire would rejuvenate heavily grazed winter range and begin regenerating aspen, an important tree to beaver and browsers. The Lava fire represented the best hope of natural fire, and the biologists cheered it on.

As tourists crowded into Yellowstone, business boomed at motels, restaurants, and T-shirt shops. A record year was underway. Inside the park, buffalo still stopped traffic and the geysers blew. But something was different about Yellowstone this year. There had been virtually no rain since Memorial Day. A drought of long standing was getting worse. The woodland that covered the 2-million-acre preserve like a dark green blanket was turning into standing kindling wood.

On July 10, as if the park had suddenly become a desert, moisture vanished in the woods. The fire danger soared. Even logs as big as a man's thigh on Mt. Sheridan were as dry as kiln-dried wood.

In that atmosphere, lightning strikes from dry summer storms were like dropping matches in Yellowstone's woods. On July 9, the Mist fire began, on the 10th, Pelican and Cone. Raven and Clover followed on the 11th, with Falls on July 12.

That was the day a fire monitor watched the Shoshone fire climb into treetops and throw embers across the channel and begin burning on the east side. For nearly two weeks the fire had sputtered, growing to sixty acres. But Perkins and the Fire Committee knew that the single leap of the river could mean trouble. Six miles away lay Grant Village, the park's newest tourist center. A hot fire could burn there in two days with the right wind. But the fire did not take off and run. The Fire Committee decided to chance it, let it go and watch it closely.

Months later, many people within the park looked back on that day with regret.

GEORGE HENLEY HAD A DOZEN VISITORS on July 14 — a crowd by a lookout's standards. He had been on the mountain nearly a month, and the wreck he'd found was now a tidy and organized home. He had hauled out of storage an old propane stove with four burners and an oven for cooking. His only chair was a director's model with a cloth back. He had a bed, a homemade table, a bench and cabinets from the 1930s, built low below the windows. His light at night came from a gas lantern. Solar panels charged the batteries for his radio and TV. He could pick up four channels from Idaho and National Public Radio from Billings, Montana.

His visitors got to see an unusual display of fire fighting. Off to the northwest beyond Shoshone Lake, smoke jumpers could be seen parachuting into the woods at the Narrows, so named for a stricture in Shoshone Lake. A backpacker had set fire to his toilet paper and touched off a wildfire. As Henley and his guests watched, an old bomber sprayed retardant.

Some of the blazes threatened ranches and houses.
The Lost Creek Ranch, in the line of the Huck Fire
which started in Grand Teton National Park,
evacuated horses and guests on "Black Saturday."
(©Ted Wood 1988)

Far to the northeast another aircraft was buzzing the Yellowstone backcountry. Dan Sholly in *H1*, the park helicopter, was looking at two remote fires high in the Lamar River drainage: the five-day-old Mist fire, now 200 acres in size, and the Clover fire, just three days old and 2,000 acres, the park's biggest fire. The Clover was flaring up that afternoon, torching treetops and moving along a fiery front.

Sholly had two concerns. The first was an outfitter in Miller Creek who needed to be evacuated with his pack horses. The second was a secret fishing trip scheduled there by Vice President George Bush. Sholly had flown to Cody, Wyoming, that morning to plan security with the Secret Service. Bush and his campaign chief, James Baker, planned to hide out in Yellowstone's backcountry during the Democratic Convention.

Bush would chopper to Frost Lake—a small, high lake in the rugged Absaroka Mountain Range that separates Yellowstone from the Shoshone National Forest—then ride horseback to Bear Lake and the Lamar River. A park crew was sprucing up the old Cold Creek patrol cabin for the vice president. They had replaced a shed roof, built a food storage cabinet, painted the floor and changed the linens.

But fire was approaching the Cache Calfee patrol cabin eight miles away. Late in the afternoon, Sholly landed with two fire aides and rushed to save the 1920s-era cabin. With the fire burning three-quarters of a mile away, they carried away a huge woodpile from the porch and scratched a fire line around the cabin, which sat in thick pine. They had no water pump and the chain saw didn't work. With flares they set fire to underbrush around the cabin to blunt the fire's force.

"The fire kept coming," said Sholly, a nationally rated fire fighter who had fought his first fire twenty-five years earlier not far from where he now was stranded. Built like a prizefighter, Sholly was the classic ranger, at ease with helicopters or horses, and sure of himself.

He had sent the chopper away. "I knew the fire would blow by. Then we could go back to the cabin if it caught fire and could put it out. If we had flown out, we'd be smoked out."

At 5:00 P.M., the fire surrounded the cabin. Sholly and the two aides retreated to a nearby meadow. In thick smoke they took cover under aluminum-coated blankets carried by fire fighters. But the trio had only two shelters. John Dunfee took one. Sholly lay with Kristen Cowan in the second. When they got up forty-five minutes later, the meadow was black except for two patches of green. The cabin was saved.

That night Yellowstone National Park Superintendent Bob Barbee called the supervisor of the Shoshone National Forest and called off Bush's Yellowstone trip. The president-to-be became the first tourist to be turned away by the fires.

Bush and Baker, with four Secret Service agents, a doctor and radio operator, instead camped and fished on the Shoshone Forest in the North Absaroka Wilderness Area. One afternoon the group rode to the ridge of the Absarokas and looked over at the fire burning in the park. By then, the Yellowstone cabin where Bush had planned to sleep was under siege. Bush was "very curious . . . about what our intentions were," said Steve Mealey, the Shoshone supervisor. "I told him that the fire was a minimum threat to the [Shoshone] forest."

By July 15, there was enough smoke and fire to be noticeable to park visitors. Yellowstone's public affairs office printed the first map of the park's fires. It listed nine fires, and on the vast square of Yellowstone most of them looked like dots. Two were less than an acre. The Clover fire was a 4,700-acre ink stain in the far reaches of the park's northeast.

The fires totaled 8,500 acres.

That much fire anywhere else in the lower forty-eight states would have been a major conflagration. Not so in Yellowstone, where the fires burned in the backcountry and the vacationing public went about its business.

Within the park administration, however, there was growing tension. Sholly organized his fire fighters into a formal structure called an incident command. On the afternoon of the 15th, they put out a lightning strike near the Tower junction because it was too close to the rustic cabins and Roosevelt Lodge. The next day a helicopter dropped off radio repeaters at Henley's lookout to improve communications between headquarters and monitors who were watching three fires in the south, the Shoshone among them.

The tension came both from within the park, as some rangers grew uneasy with the amount of fire, and from outside, as colleagues in the national forests around Yellowstone began fighting fires. Like Yellowstone, the forests had natural-fire policies in designated wilderness areas adjoining the park. Fires were even allowed to burn across the border, from the park into a forest, or vice versa.

But if the woods got too dry, as measured by fire-danger calculations, or if commercial stands of timber were threatened, fires in the national forests were suppressed. That began happening July 2 in the Gallatin National Forest, north of Yellowstone, where a lightning fire called Storm Creek had burned since June 14. To the west, on July 12, the Targhee National Forest notified Yellowstone that because of severe drought, it did not want any park fires to burn across the border. On July 14, the supervisor of the Bridger-Teton Forest, to the south, declared the three-day-old Mink fire wild. On July 17, Yellowstone began backburns to keep the Falls fire from crossing the boundary into the Targhee Forest.

Smoke was increasingly hazing the views, and the smell of burning wood wafted through

On the leading edge of the Mink fire, a pine tree torches. (©Ted Wood 1988)

Fire fighters were
organized into groups,
each with a leader. Here
the Mormon Lake Hot
Shots, a crew from
Flagstaff, Arizona, head
into a wilderness area
where they were only
allowed to use hand
tools to combat the
blazes. (©Ted Wood
1988)

Starting a backburn.
(©Jeff Henry 1988)

the park each day. An enormous burnout set by fire fighters on the Mink fire sent a convection cloud 30,000 feet into the air and released 3.5 trillion BTUs per hour, enough to heat 4,400 homes for a year. In the Lamar Valley, students at the Yellowstone Institute sat on the porch at dusk and watched the red fireballs of tree crowns burning on the Clover-Mist far up the river. Park rangers watched it, too, as fascinated as anyone by a natural forest fire burning unhindered. Some were vocal. During the informal meetings of the Fire Committee, there was often heated discussion about the wisdom of letting the fires burn. Increasingly, complaints were being heard from tourists and neighbors.

On July 20, the Shoshone fire burned two miles toward Grant Village, pushed by high winds. Perkins and the fire bosses in the park began writing a fire fighting plan. The next day they declared the Red, Shoshone and Falls fires wild.

What no one knew, in or out of the park, was that on that day, Yellowstone was tipping rapidly toward crisis. On July 21, as if an angry God played his hand, Yellowstone's smoldering fires erupted.

The Clover and Mist fires joined hands and made a run for the eastern border, bumping against the talus slopes of the Absaroka Range. At Frost Lake, it threatened to burn into the North Absaroka Wilderness. Mealey, the Shoshone supervisor, reversed his position and told Yellowstone officials he did not want the fire to burn on the forest because it could not be stopped once it crossed the divide. "They didn't see the danger I did," said Mealey.

Yellowstone had no choice but to declare the fire wild and begin to fight it. Crews were dispatched to the rugged region.

The Shoshone fire, meanwhile, edged closer to Grant Village, a modern shake-shingled, tourist center on the shores of Yellowstone Lake. The campground was full and the motels were busy.

On the same day, the Red fire bulged around the south side of Lewis Lake and headed toward the lake campground. As Gary Brown, the assistant chief ranger, watched, the Red showed unusual behavior, burning against the wind through an old previously burned area. "We began to wonder and wonder. And when it went toward the south end of the lake and roared, in my mind, things were different."

About 11:00 P.M. that night, the phone rang in Dave Poncin's home in Grangeville, Idaho. Poncin, a jowly, jovial man of fifty-one, was one of a handful of men considered to be the country's top fire fighters. He led one of eighteen Class 1 overhead fire fighting teams. By midnight Poncin was en route to Missoula, Montana, where at 5:00 A.M. he rendezvoused with the rest of his team, men who had worked together for years fighting fires. At 6 A.M., they flew to West Yellowstone, had breakfast and were briefed on the fires. They arrived at Grant Village that afternoon. What they saw, Poncin would never forget.

"The wind was blowing smoke right into Grant Village. Ash was falling around us." The village and campground were filled with thousands of tourists and employees.

Dead wood lay on the ground in huge piles, some up against the wood motels, each of them tinder boxes with huge cedar shake roofs. "My blood ran cold," Poncin said. "I was standing there in the smoke, looking at the buildings, and wondering, 'How could they do it?' It was looking pretty grim that first evening."

Park Superintendent Bob Barbee gave Poncin three jobs: save Grant Village and the campground at Lewis Lake and keep the Falls fire in the park.

Poncin and his crew set up camp on the lakeshore and took stock. Grant Village contained a 1-million gallon water tank and hydrants around the buildings. Two hundred fifty fire fighters and several fire engines had arrived. But no one knew how much time they had to prepare for the fire headed their way.

A backburn was started along the main park road at Grant Village to try to stop the advancing fire. By eliminating the fuel, the theory is that the fire won't be able to move forward. A fire coordinator keeps track by radio of the fire movements up and down the road. This backburn didn't work. The flames jumped the road. Grant Village was the first major fire fight, and it gave fire fighters a bitter taste of what they were up against. (©Ted Wood 1988)

A huge cloud rises above
the Mink fire, the first
large fire in the
Yellowstone Ecosystem.
(©Ted Wood 1988)

Fire Policy

THE IDEA OF LETTING FIRES BURN naturally grew from the same seeds that sprouted the green revolution, wilderness protection and the science of ecology—the recognition that all living things are connected.

In the 1950s, managers of the Everglades National Park began setting fires to open glades and piney woods to benefit wildlife. In the 1960s, studies recommended that other national parks try to represent vignettes of primitive America. The Leopold Report of 1963 argued that despite a history of heavy use by man, parks should try to recreate a "reasonable illusion" of natural regulation.

In Yellowstone, wildness had gradually been accorded greater respect and freedom. Wolves, who had been shot in the 1930s, were now recognized for their role in the food chain. Hot springs no longer were channeled for swimming pools, and bears were weaned from garbage and forced to forage naturally.

Fire, it was reasoned, helped create the ecosystem and its absence meant an unnatural system.

In 1972, Yellowstone adopted a plan to let lightning fires burn in backcountry areas. National forests around the park were slower to respond to the philosophy. They had traditionally put fires out. But as wilderness areas were created within U.S. forests, they, too, adopted rules to let fires burn.

The rules had a special language. Fires could burn under guidelines called a *prescription*. When a fire exceeded the prescription, it was declared wild and suppressed.

In Yellowstone, lightning fires were in prescription anywhere except along the park's boundary and around the tourist centers. Under the plan, fires would be fought if they threatened life or property, or if they were started by humans.

Yellowstone stood alone in not putting preestablished limits on their fires—"trigger" points when fires would be declared wild and fought. Neighboring forests, for example, limited fires to 1,000 acres, or began to fight them when fuel moistures dipped below a certain level. Low moistures make controlling a fire difficult.

Yellowstone's fire managers said that arbitrary triggers meant that fires would be put out before they did ecologic good, and ran contrary to the basic philosophy of natural management. As one park scientist put it, placing limits on natural fire was tantamount to saying "nature is good only to a point."

In Yellowstone, decisions on each fire were left to a Fire Committee whose members were committed to letting fires burn. They, in turn, advised the superintendent, who made the final decision to fight a fire or let it go.

As the summer of 1988 began to unfold, triggers went off in the national forests all around Yellowstone, and fires there were fought one to three weeks before they were fought in Yellowstone. Several fires in the park were put out because they were too close to tourist areas or to neighboring forests that did not want them. Not until July 21, when fire raced toward Grant Village, were the first lightning fires declared wild in Yellowstone.

During the Summer of Fire, thirty-one fires were allowed to burn as prescribed fires in the Greater Yellowstone Ecosystem, twenty-eight of them in Yellowstone Park. Of the twenty-eight, twelve burned less than an acre. The other sixteen were eventually declared wildfires and burned out of control. One prescribed fire in the Custer National Forest and one in the Bridger-Teton National Forest blew out of control.

Fire fighters watch as an entire ridge south of Canyon Village goes up in flame. They are also on guard for spot fires. (©Ted Wood 1988)

Fire history

A BIRD ON THE WING HAS THE best view of Yellowstone's fiery past—and how fire has shaped the park.

Vast, even stands of lodgepole pine stretch from one end of the park to the other. Some stands are young, others old and broken. The woods are interrupted by meadows. Sage steppes cover the northern range. Each landscape is home to different birds and animals. The very diversity of Yellowstone is due to fire.

Fire has swept the land periodically since the last ice age 12,000 years ago. Fire killed old growth and prepared the ground for a new crop. The trees grew up uniform in height, then aged and died. Another fire repeated the cycle. Scientists estimate that major fires burned across Yellowstone every 100 to 400 years. Some ancient trees show scars from 1525. Major fires swept large parts of the park in the early 1700s and 1850.

But there is fire every year, thanks to lightning. Summer thunderstorms create thousands of strikes. Eighty percent fizzle out. Since 1930, there have been 1,298 fires, 57 percent of them lightning-caused.

Since 1972, under the natural fire program, lightning set 235 fires in Yellowstone, most of them burning less than an acre, but four ranged from 1,000 to 3,500 acres. In sixteen years lightning fires burned 34,157 acres.

Fire keeps meadows and wooded areas in balance. Old stands of lodgepole (80 to 100 years is old) become infected with dwarf mistletoe and mountain pine beetle. The trees die and fall, creating fuel buildup for future fires. Spruce and fir grow between the old lodgepole and become "ladder" fuels. Half the park was in this condition when the fires started in 1988.

Fires also create a mosaic of different-aged trees that prevent the spread of infestations. If fires are put out, tree stands become uniform and susceptible to disease.

Many species are adapted to fire. Douglas fir has a thick bark to survive flames. Rabbitbrush and aspen spring to life after fires. Fireweed, appropriately named, is often the first plant to reestablish itself in ash.

But in Yellowstone, the most dramatic sight is the opening of the lodgepole pinecone after a fire. Serotinous pinecones are tightly closed until heat evaporates the pitch and allows cells at the base of the cone to dry and contract. The cones open and the seeds fall out. Shortly after a fire there are 10,000 to 50,000 seeds per acre.

Long before the fires were out in Yellowstone, new shoots of green poked through the black ash. Plant growth is triggered by increased minerals and light. About twenty species of plants resprout, including lupine, leafy aster, elk sedge and heart-leafed arnica. The growth of willows, serviceberry, chokeberry, mountain ash and other plants also is stimulated by fire.

Within three years burned ground is 70 percent covered with new plant life. This new growth, in turn, attracts animals. Large animals such as elk, bears, coyotes and moose increase after fires. Small animals such as deer mice, although killed in large numbers by fire, mushroom afterward. Coyotes, foxes, mountain lions and bears follow the small mammals into the regrowth. And grizzlies love berry plants that resprout after fire.

Some birds are driven away by fire, but other species, including raptors and cavity nesters like mountain bluebirds, come back.

Fish spawning areas are hurt by siltation after fires, but the nutrients in the ash and increased organic material that wash into the streams increases aquatic productivity.

Fireweed, appropriately named, is often the first plant to reestablish itself in ash. (©Jeff Henry 1988)

By September, new grasses were already appearing near Grant Village, where just two months earlier fires had scoured the area. (©Ted Wood 1988)

T HE FIRE SITUATION CONTINUES TO BE critical," Henley wrote July 22. "The Shoshone fire is approaching Grant Village. The Red jumped the road south of Lewis Falls and is heading east. Rain fell for thirty seconds."

While Henley watched, the Lewis Lake campground was closed and the Shoshone fire ran a hot finger toward Grant Village, bursting to 1,000 acres. Fire leaped from treetop to treetop. Poncin knew he had to evacuate.

The news shook the park like an earthquake. The tourist season was at its peak. Grant Village was filled with 3,000 visitors and employees. Finding room for them would be a nightmare. And news of an evacuation could turn other people away from Yellowstone.

There was also the unspoken thought among many in the park: how had it come to this?

"No one was believing this," said Sholly. "People said, 'You've got to be kidding.' "

As the tour buses pulled out, Poncin's lieutenants went to work with trucks and backhoes to pick up tons

Throughout the summer, fire fighters doused hot spots in an effort to keep fires from spreading. (©Ted Wood 1988)

of dead wood that had lain on the ground since Grant Village was built in the 1960s. Poncin wanted a 150-foot barrier around the buildings. Others with chain saws began cutting the lower limbs of trees, the "ladder fuels" that fire climbs into the treetops.

"It's not easy to wait until the fire challenges us," Poncin told crews chomping to fight the fire where it burned. He asked them to think about the park's natural fire policy. "We're privileged to take part in a historic event."

As his sawyers worked Friday afternoon, another woodcutter worked alone miles to the west, filling his pickup with firewood for the winter. He cut in an old logging area in the Targhee National Forest, 200 yards from Yellowstone's western boundary. He smoked, too, and dropped a cigarette into the duff at his feet and drove away, not knowing what he had started. The dry grass burst into flames and the fire spread into blowdown and beetle-killed lodgepole pine.

Within an hour a fire alarm sounded in the Island Park Ranger Station, and four pumper trucks raced up the gravel logging roads. The fire had burned up a slope through woods toward the park. The wind was blowing strong, and within two hours the fire was 150 feet wide and moving rapidly in a long, thin strip into Yellowstone. The fire was called the North Fork.

Rodd Richardson, the Island Park ranger, radioed for smoke jumpers from nearby West Yellowstone, Montana, and four bulldozers from logging crews in the area. As the smoke jumpers flew over, they reported the fire at seventy-five acres, burning in the park, and the wind at 25 to 40 mph, too strong to jump. Bulldozers began digging a perimeter line around the fire.

The same wind raced across Yellowstone, pushing fire wherever it burned. Near Lewis Lake a bizarre downburst from a convection column broke and uprooted trees along three miles of the south entrance road. On the eastern front, the Clover-Mist ballooned to 31,500

acres and broke over the Absaroka Range at Canoe Lake and Frost Lake. Two more national fire teams were called.

Larry Caplinger, thirty-one years in fire fighting and a blunt, no-nonsense Class 1 leader from central California, was called to the North Fork fire, by now four miles into the park and 1,300 acres. At the fire's rear, on the Targhee National Forest, bulldozers had dug a line around the fire, up the hill onto the Madison Plateau. But at the border park officials had drawn a line. There would be no bulldozers in Yellowstone. Their scars would outlast any fire. In the park fire fighters were to go "light on the land" with hand tools.

Caplinger was frustrated. Used to fighting fires in California with all-out strategies, he wanted to circle the North Fork with a bulldozer and stop it at 1,500 acres on the flat, timbered plain, a good place to control a fire. But with fire more an imminent peril at Grant Village, Caplinger's work and crews were second priority. By Saturday night he received orders to back off and let the fire burn in the park. It would be watched by helicopter.

Meanwhile, Kurt Bates, a twenty-five-year fire fighting veteran from Glenwood Springs, Colorado, tall and ruggedly western, was dispatched to Cody, Wyoming, to stop the Clover-Mist on the Shoshone National Forest. He was to let it go in the park, where it was burning intensely in dead, tumbled wood. On the Shoshone, lines were built and backburns set. With smoke jumpers and retardant drops, the team made quick progress.

Yellowstone's fire map now showed eleven fires, totaling 46,000 acres, but the focus was on three: the Clover-Mist, the North Fork and the Red-Shoshone-Fan, now called the Snake River Complex. There were 500 fire fighters on duty and another 250 en route. On July 23, an Area Command was established in West Yellowstone to coordinate fire fighting.

"The smoke," Henley wrote, "is starting to block the sun." Indeed, Yellowstone's smoke now was visible 500 miles away, in Casper and

Cheyenne, Wyoming.

On Sunday, July 24, the North Fork fire leaped five miles directly toward the centerpiece of Yellowstone National Park. "Fire roars toward Old Faithful," read the headline in the *Denver Post*. It was electrifying news.

The fire was nine miles away from the visitor complex. Ash fell around tourists and buildings, including the historic log Old Faithful Inn. A huge pillar of smoke was visible to the west, a grim backdrop to the eruptions of the famous geyser.

Area Command recommended that the complex be closed, but Bob Barbee, the genial general of Yellowstone, balked. He still had time to evacuate. But a park spokesman announced that visitors should reconsider their trips to Yellowstone. "These are condi-tions that we haven't seen in the recorded his-tory of Yellowstone," said the spokesman.

From a practical standpoint, the threat to Old Faithful was minimal. The geyser had long ago been surrounded by parking lots and cin-der lawns and there was no danger to the gey-ser itself. But each day 25,000 people visited the geyser, the main attraction in Yellowstone. Just the thought of the icon in a wildfire was symbolic and disturbing.

Caplinger and his crew moved to Old Faithful at midnight, followed by the national news media.

As fireproofing began in an orange pall, reporters discovered the Snake River fires spewing towering clouds of orange, gray, black and white. Fire teams hosed down build-ings at Lewis Lake. At West Thumb, Alice and

The Shoshone fire headed toward Grant Village. On July 25, after Grant had been evac-uated, fire fighters and equipment lined the main road about a quarter mile west of the village to try to stop the advancing wall of flame. But the fire jumped the road and raced toward the campground where the fire camp was set up. All fire personnel were evacuated to the Yellowstone lakeshore. (©Ted Wood 1988)

By mid-July there were 500 fire fighters on duty and another 250 en route. An area command was established in West Yellowstone to coordinate fire fighting. (©Ted Wood 1988)

Putting out fires with hand tools was exhausting work. (©Ted Wood 1988)

too smokey for helicopter drops of slurry. That was spectacular to me."

Inside the camp, lime green structural engines with enormous water pressure patrolled the loops. As forty-foot-high fire boiled into the crowns of trees, the engine crews sprayed huge gushes of water. Again and again they knocked the flame from the trees. "I've never seen that before," said Poncin. "It was a big-eyed experience."

Charlie Rising Sun was pumping gas for fire trucks when the flames seared through the lodgepole by his Conoco service station, where a propane tank sat exposed. He shut down the pumps as a four-engine bomber roared overhead, dropping gooey, pink slurry to keep the flames from igniting an inferno. Slurry dripped from the phone booth windows and from picnic tables nearby. The fire burned to within a few feet of the propane tank and laundry building.

On loop L of the campground, the fire blackened the drive-ins and scorched a restroom, breaking the glass windows. It also burned holes in some tents in the camp. But the fire abated, the caterer moved back from the shoreline, and by 7:00 P.M. dinner was served. During the dramatic day, fifteen fire fighters had been injured slightly.

Except for the restroom, everything was saved at Grant Village. Crews moved in to mop up, the drudge work of turning over smokey soil and roots, washing each one with water until dead out. Fire still burned in pockets and smoke hung like fog when journalists were allowed in. Near the blackened bathroom, a dead squirrel lay, its tail burned off. Next to it, several lodgepole pinecones, open from the heat, lay exposed. They were beginning to scatter their seeds.

That night, George Henley had trouble sleeping in the smoke. Whether it was a bad dream or real, he awoke with the feeling that he was out of breath and gasping. The next morning a helicopter picked him up, and carried him off the mountain.

Phil Winn, a retired couple working in Hamilton's tiny convenience store, evacuated. TV cameras showed them loading liquor and other valuables into station wagons and driving away in the smoke.

On the afternoon of July 25, Dave Poncin stood in the road outside Grant Village when the fire front hit. "It went over the top of us. You'd look down the highway and there would be a thousand little fires burning on the asphalt. We caught many of them, but a half mile in, the hoses couldn't reach, and it was

Four-engine bombers made drops of slurry, a type of nitrogen fertilizer colored pink for visibility, to keep the flames from igniting an inferno. (©Ted Wood 1988)

By late July and early August, tourists throughout the park and in neighboring towns were well aware of the fires. A park spokesman announced that visitors should reconsider their trips to Yellowstone. (©Ted Wood 1988)

This fire fighter is mopping up—doing the drudge work of turning over smokey soil and roots, washing each with water until the fire is dead out. (©Ted Wood 1988)

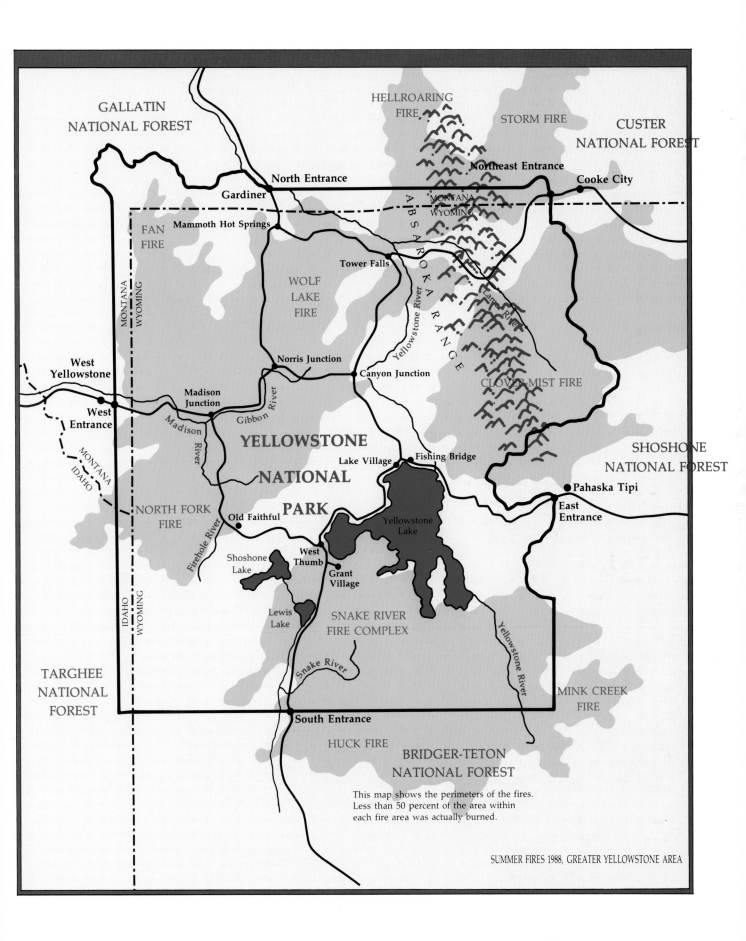

GALLATIN
NATIONAL FOREST

CUSTER
NATIONAL FOREST

HELLROARING
FIRE

STORM FIRE

North Entrance

Northeast Entrance

Cooke City

Gardiner

FAN
FIRE

Mammoth Hot Springs

MONTANA
WYOMING

West
Yellowstone

WOLF
LAKE
FIRE

Tower Falls

A B S A R O K A   R A N G E

Yellowstone River

CLOVER-MIST FIRE

MONTANA
WYOMING

Norris Junction

Canyon Junction

West
Entrance

Madison
Junction

Gibbon River

SHOSHONE
NATIONAL FOREST

Madison River

YELLOWSTONE

MONTANA
IDAHO

Lake Village

Fishing Bridge

NATIONAL

Pahaska Tipi

NORTH FORK
FIRE

Old Faithful

PARK

*Yellowstone
Lake*

East
Entrance

Firehole River

Shoshone
Lake

West
Thumb

Grant
Village

Lewis
Lake

SNAKE RIVER
FIRE COMPLEX

IDAHO
WYOMING

Snake River

Yellowstone River

MINK CREEK
FIRE

TARGHEE
NATIONAL
FOREST

South Entrance

HUCK FIRE

BRIDGER-TETON
NATIONAL FOREST

This map shows the perimeters of the fires.
Less than 50 percent of the area within
each fire area was actually burned.

SUMMER FIRES 1988, GREATER YELLOWSTONE AREA

Ecologist Don Despain

A HORNTAIL WASP FLEW PAST Don Despain's head, looking for a freshly killed lodgepole pine tree.

"She'll deposit her eggs an inch deep in the trunk," said Despain. "Come back next summer and pull back the bark. It will be crawling with larvae—round-headed wood bores."

Despain stepped over a log that was burning at one end.

"The happiest little pine seedling I've seen was in a fire. It had long, luxurious needles. It was really growing."

Despain, forty-seven, is Yellowstone's fire lover, a research biologist who spent seventeen years waiting for a fire season like 1988. He kicked through ashes of a three-day-old blaze. "In 1981, we had a good year. We burned 20,000 acres."

In 1972, Despain helped write the park's natural fire policy and remained its philosophic torchbearer. "I don't like suppression efforts," he said.

At the height of Yellowstone's fires, with 400,000 acres burned, Despain led research crews to the front of the fires to lay out test plots 15 by 25 meters ahead of the flames. They recorded all vegetation in the plot, and then planned to check it year after year.

"Most people who watch TV think the trees are burned up," he said. "They are not. These are the future homes of wood-digesting fungi, which are food for insects. And bears and birds eat insects." He waved his arm at a stark scene, dead trees, black ground, ashes piled on ashes. "From the eyes of a wood bore this is a feast laid out. And so it's a feast for woodpeckers."

He crossed a fire line and picked a spot, drove stakes and began the survey. The jetlike sound of fires crowning grew frequent. On the ground the fires nibbled closer. "Timber," someone yelled, and a burning tree fell.

The group stopped for lunch, and as Despain drilled core samples sparks began falling around him. He wore an aluminum helmet over steel gray hair, striped suspenders and a yellow shirt. He smiled a toothy grin.

A wall of fire roared to the left. Spots of smoke appeared in the sedge by the Gibbon River—the escape route. Despain pulled a blue kerchief to his nose, put goggles on and balanced across a fallen log over the Gibbon River.

In seconds sparks had ignited rug-sized fires in front of him. Smoke swirled and he disappeared. "This is the first time I've seen one of my plots burn. Burn, baby, burn."

He sat on a log across the river and watched the flames.

"After three years, the amount of ground cover on the forest floor will equal prefire levels." The fires also open endless research possibilities—like insect regeneration and the effect of smoke on plants in unburned areas.

"If we had put the fires out," said Despain, "we'd have missed what happens in these extreme years. The politicians will say you don't need to know."

He started to walk back, then bent to show dozens of lodgepole seeds in the ash, next to elk and chipmunk tracks.

"If fires like this can't burn every 200 years, Yellowstone won't be a natural park. It will be a museum piece, and as time goes on it will be more dangerous. Grant Village is now protected from fire for 200 years. I think what happened this year should have happened."

Stark aftermath of the North Fork fire. (©Jeff Henry 1988)

From seemingly barren land, new growth begins almost immediately, with each type of plant taking hold in its season. This photograph was taken in 1985 of an area that burned five years earlier. The ground is covered with foliage and low-growing bushes are spreading. (©Jeff Henry 1988)

By NOW THE WORLD HAD DISCOVERED the Yellowstone fires. Tall columns of flame filled television screens, accompanied by sound tracks of malicious crackling. Newspapers ran front-page pictures of yellow-clad fire fighters dwarfed by the orange and red. "Fires Rage in Yellowstone," was a typical headline.

The smoke was so thick tourists drove with their lights on. A few complained. A few coughed.

"Smoking or nonsmoking?" a hostess giggled at the haze-filled Old Faithful Inn dining room. "Oh, I guess it really doesn't make any difference, does it?" Everyone waiting in line had an opinion.

"I think it is a fine policy. It clears out the forest and lets it go through a natural cycle," said Shirley Holle of Boulder, Colorado.

"I wanted to cry," said Barb Canale of Syracuse, New York. "It's part of America being destroyed. I understand the rejuvenation and all, but still it's sad to see the park burn down."

But those who had traveled so far to see Yellowstone continued to pour into the park. As they paid the

Like soldiers marching in formation, these Hot Shots head off on patrol to look for "spots," small flareups in advance of the main fire. (©Ted Wood 1988)

Tourists traveled through the haze with their lights on. Toward the end of August, they were ushered toward the exits in caravans. (©Ted Wood 1988)

$10 fee, they were handed a pamphlet saying they were "fortunate" to witness a natural process:

> Over thousands of years, lightning fires have been one of the important natural processes that have shaped the forests of Yellowstone. Much of the park is covered with lodgepole pine that grew after past fires. Studies have found these trees burn every 300 to 400 years. So, in a sense, we're seeing history being made.

Still, there was the growing impression that something was wrong in the world's first national park.

"The vast majority of the public calling in think that the national treasure is being lost," said George Robinson, the chief of interpretation. The truth was that only 3 percent of the 2 million acres was afire.

"Charred forests are a hard sell," said Superintendent Barbee. "Smokey the Bear led people to conclude that all fires are bad. Right now it looks like a celestial war took place. In a few years, it will be a carpet of new growth."

Conditioned by Smokey—"only you can prevent forest fires"—by Bambi, fire drills, by a million years of acculturation of fire, the flames in Yellowstone cut through to something basic—fear. The politicians were the first to react.

"We're hearing from people today, saying 'put the damn thing out,' " said a press secretary to Wyoming Senator Malcolm Wallop. As Poncin's crew made its back-to-the-wall save in Grant Village, Wallop was on the phone in Washington to Interior Secretary Don Hodel, the Park Service boss. Smoke was drifting into Cody and Jackson and tourist business was down. At Flagg Ranch, a resort near the closed south entrance, business was off 40 percent.

Hodel told the senator that the park would suppress any new fires, and that the sixteen-year-old policy of letting fires burn would be reexamined because of the unprecedented drought.

Tourist gets a bird's-eye view of the North Fork fire from a telephone tower in West Yellowstone, Montana. (©Jeff Henry 1988)

The Lava fire near Mammoth was the first political victim. When it was announced that Hodel would visit the park July 27, Barbee ordered fire fighters to surround the 60-acre fire and stomp it out. "Don't want more big ones," the fire map declared.

During visits to Old Faithful and Grant Village, the interior secretary repeated his promise to douse new fires, but said large fires already burning would have a "long-term beneficial effect."

Three hundred people from Gardiner, Montana, signed a petition presented to Hodel, demanding a change in fire policy. They complained of smoke and a drop in tourism.

But Poncin, at Grant, agreed with Hodel. "It is very easy, where there is a lot of smoke, to react to political or nonbiologic information. After the heat of battle, we should review the summer of 1988 and see whether the burn strategy is good or evil."

Hodel saw the park during a lull in fire activity, but nearly every day new fires were discovered. The board in the fire cache now listed thirty-four fires. Eleven were major fronts, and 1,500 fire fighters were on nine. Fires covered 88,000 acres.

The Clover-Mist fire, at 68,000 acres in the park, had met its match on the Shoshone side of the mountains. On July 27, after two days of digging hand lines and dropping slurry, Bates' team stopped the slopover at 1,200 acres.

Near Old Faithful, fire-spitting helicopters went to war against the North Fork fire. The napalmlike fuel burned trees in front of the fire to divert it away from the geyser. As tourists watched the air show, the park announced that, for now, Old Faithful was safe.

"It would be extraordinary if Old Faithful was threatened again by this fire," said Park Service spokesman Costa Dillon.

At Grant Village, truck-mounted flame throwers ignited big piles of underbrush and timber, and Poncin extended the burnout buffer to three-fourths of a mile. The Park prepared to reopen the village to tourists. The Shoshone continued to nag, though, and the West Thumb convenience store was evacuated and reopened like a yoyo for several days.

The Lewis Lake campground was secure and crews cut hazardous, half-burned trees that hung precariously near the roads and trails. Lookout Henley helped reconstruct an osprey nest that fell over with a burned tree by the lake. An osprey chick had been found with a broken leg, his parents gone. A splint was placed on the leg, and a new nest erected in another tree. Henley and biologists caught fish, tore them into strips and put the meat into the nest. Other osprey chicks died in the fire, but the parents of Henley's rescued bird returned. On Saturday, July 30, a helicopter returned Henley to his nest on Mt. Sheridan.

In West Yellowstone, Montana, area commanders used the lull to take stock. Expenses were mounting. With 100,000 acres burned, the Yellowstone fires had cost $3.4 million.

Yellowstone was not the only fire in the West, either. Utah, Montana, Idaho, South Dakota, California, Washington, Wisconsin and Alaska all reported fires, many near communities. Under the nation's fire-fighting rules, life and property took top priority for fire fighters, helicopters and slurry bombers. Resources were stretched. What, the fire bosses wanted to know, did the future hold at Yellowstone?

Dick Rothermel, known as the nation's fire-behavior guru, arrived at West Yellowstone with a computer under his arm to help answer that question. Rothermel, fifty-nine, had virtually invented the science of fire behavior at the U.S. Forest Service Intermountain Fire Lab in Missoula. In 1961, with aeronautic engineering experience, he had begun working with fires in wind tunnels, and by 1967 was teaching fire behavior to fire crews nationwide. Among his developments were a computer program small enough for a hand-held calculator that fire bosses could carry into the woods to predict fire behavior for the next day.

Rothermel knew there was enormous risk in looking beyond twelve hours. But he could guess at "probable" fire behavior based on weather forecasts and how trees in front of the fires might burn. Don Despain, the rumpled ideologue of fire ecology in the park, had mapped the entire park, practically tree by tree. From cramped quarters in an old fishing store, Rothermel, Despain and four colleagues worked late into the night, and presented their findings to a gathering of all the fire bosses on August 2.

Their forecast was optimistic. Yellowstone's fires would grow 25 to 50 percent if they were left alone. The North Fork fire, already diverted from Old Faithful, would not reach Madison Junction, where the Gibbon and Firehole rivers form the Madison. There were too many young fuels in the way, and Despain's records showed that fire died in those fuels.

The Fan fire would hold at the park's northern border, because of the rugged barrier provided by the Gallatin Range. The Falls fire would hold at the southern end. The Mink fire, burning in the Bridger-Teton wilderness, would burn into the park but do no harm. The Shoshone fire, by then nibbling at the edge of Yellowstone Lake, would not be a problem. And the Clover-Mist, the huge ink blot on the park's eastern wilderness, would stay contained by the Absaroka Range, the jagged edge of mountaintops that marked the park's meandering eastern boundary.

Rothermel's projections were vital to decisions then being made by Superintendent Barbee. On the three major fires, the incident commanders had prepared options for him, ranging from let burn to full control. All three fire bosses estimated that with enough money and manpower, they could control the fires they were fighting. But it was the park's decision.

The team headed by Curt Bates prepared

During his late July visit to the park, Interior Secretary Don Hodel promised that new fires would be doused, but said that fires already burning would have a long-term beneficial effect. (©Jeff Henry 1988)

options on the Clover-Mist. Although the fire was controlled on one border crossing, it was running free-rein on the north, south and west. Option A called for monitoring the fire and allowing it to burn to the natural mountain breaks. The cost would be $52,000 and have a 60-percent chance of success. Option B called for forty fire fighters to fight for a week and mop up a second week. Helicopters would be used for a cost of $377,000 and an 80-percent chance of success. Option C would have thrown 600 people into the fight at a cost

A soldier, one of the army troops assigned to the Yellowstone fires, takes a break after clearing debris and trees surrounding a power substation. (©Ted Wood 1988)

of $2 million but with a 90-percent chance of success.

In his journal, written while his men contained the fire's slopover on the Shoshone National Forest, Bates wrote of the frustration he felt working under park rules. "It is almost impossible to prevent a fire this large from crossing over the boundary without constructing lines and attacking it on the park side." Bates accepted the rules, but as a fire fighter trained to put out fire, found it difficult to wait on a ridge until fire reached him.

Barbee chose the least expensive option on the Clover-Mist. There had been moderation in burning, and he would "accept calculated risk of self-confinement at this time."

Bates agreed with assessments that the fire probably would hold in its natural boundaries, but he left the fire August 2 uneasy. "We left knowing that what action we had taken had not solved the problem. There was still a big fire."

The same sort of decision was made on the North Fork fire, where Larry Caplinger had pushed to put men and machines on fragile land west of Old Faithful. The first proposal, costing $500,000, would let the fire burn untended and require fire fighters to make a stand at Old Faithful. The second, $2-million, idea, was to turn the fire with helicopters and let it burn freely to the north. If it got to the Madison River, fire fighters would stop it on the cliffs over the river. The third would put a bulldozer line around the front of the fire at a cost of $4 million and two or three lives. Based on the Rothermel forecast, the second option was chosen and burnouts begun.

Dave Poncin, who had successfully fended the fire at West Thumb, Grant Village and Lewis Lake, presented similar options with costs estimates. The decision there, too, was to hold the line and not attack the fires aggressively. Poncin agreed. "With quick, aggressive attack we could have put them out. But you have to realize the park was under a natural fire program."

Fire Fighting

LIKE A WAR, THE GRUNTS AT THE front took the beating. You could see it on their faces after hours on the line. Smudged and weary, they even carried their tools like GIs, over their shoulders.

Their reward was their pay, $100–225 a day, because Yellowstone gave them little to be proud of as fire fighters. They spent the day scratching line in the duff, and the next watching fire burn over it.

At night they slept on the ground, in the smoke that lay like a blanket on the fire camps, acrid and thick. Food was good, and there was plenty of it. Usually.

The Redding, California, Hot Shots didn't get supper the first night they set up their spike camp. They had to sleep on a hot spring, wrapped in space blankets. The third night, they missed supper again, so they divided what they had. Most got a slice of bread and two grapes. By their fifth day they were looking for grouse to butcher. Because a helicopter couldn't land in smoke, they fought sixteen hours a day for five days on five meals. When they finally got out, half the crew had bronchitis or was coughing.

And then they learned that all the line they had built, the line west of Old Faithful, was being abandoned. They couldn't hold it. The wind was blowing, and throwing sparks well beyond their puny scratches.

"I'll always remember Yellowstone," said Curt Sattler of Folsom, California, "knowing there was nothing we could do to stop these fires."

At the fire-fighting peak, nearly 10,000 fire fighters were on the lines in and around Yellowstone. They faced incredible danger—fire storms, 200-foot walls of flame, grizzly bears, buffalo, sulphur rocks that spit acid when sprayed with water. Bears rummaged in their garbage. Helicopters were kept in corrals to prevent dam-

The work of fire fighting went on at camp, too, where tools had to be sharpened daily so that the hand tool method of going "light on the land" would be productive. (©Jeff Henry 1988)

age from bison. Falling trees injured many, and killed one fire fighter.

And under the Park's rules, most of the work was by hand—grunt work.

"Park values is the point," said Chief Ranger Dan Sholly. "If we had allowed bulldozers there would be 300 miles of bulldozer line," visible long after the burned forests healed. The park resisted what Sholly called the southern California mentality—aggressive, damaging action, with dozers and trucks to stop a fire. That may be needed outside a city like Los Angeles, but not in Yellowstone. The fire crews played by Yellowstone's rules, even if it bridled them. It was a challenge to many. They felt good working hard in an important place.

"Fighting fires has changed my life," said Francis Trujillo, on guard with his Pulaski on a fire line. "I used to do alcohol and drugs. Now I feel good. With this money, I'm buying things for my family."

Trujillo is a Laguna Pueblo Indian. He and his crew were cutting line to stop a fire from spreading toward Canyon Village. A spark landed at his feet and Trujillo buried the "smoke" in the dirt, a drop of fire in an ocean of flame.

Across a valley, fire blew like a wind tunnel through the tops of trees, toward the Yellowstone River. As they dug their line, it leaped the river. Trujillo's radio clicked on.

"You guys saved the village, but we lost the war," said a voice.

Victory was a small job well done in a tiny corner of Yellowstone.

THOUGH SMOTHERED IN SMOKE AS AUGUST began, Yellowstone maintained its enduring qualities. In the haze buffalo grazed, the geysers erupted more or less on schedule, and there was a sense, argued strongly by the park service, that fires—even the crisis they caused—were part of the landscape. At Grant Village, where flames flickered alongside the road and mop-up crews with kerchiefs to their noses stomped through hot ashes with hoses, park naturalists led walks into the worst of it and talked of better days. Soon, said Barbara Pettinga, elk would return to lick minerals released by the fire. By next year, mountain bluebirds would return. Lupine would blossom; fireweed, mallow and mushrooms would grow. The black, she said, was a fertilizer.

Across the park, there was a growing sense, too, that the fires were abating. "Yellowstone fires begin to calm" one paper proclaimed. With 200,000 acres burned in Yellowstone, William Penn Mott, the director of the National Park Service, wrote to Wyoming's Senator Wallop: "I am pleased to report that with the help of

An elk, undisturbed by the thick blanket of smoke surrounding it, goes about his normal grazing in the Elk Park area along the Gibbon River. (©Ted Wood 1988)

some 2,000-plus fire fighters and professional staff, all Yellowstone area fires are under control, and unless an extreme weather event, such as continuous high winds, occurs, we expect them to remain so."

From his Mt. Sheridan lookout, Henley could see that 1988's fires, though off the front page, were not out.

"Rain fell five minutes," he wrote on August 1. "Red Fire came within a quarter mile of Heart Lake Cabin." On August 2: "Red burned into the old fire. It edged around the north and east sides of the mountains, and burned below a cliff."

Each day the fire maps showed creeping growth in the backcountry. The weather remained hot and dry. The park now had gone two months with virtually no rain. And August brought dry, cold fronts with the added menace of wind.

On August 1, a front blew through Yellowstone with 40-mph winds. Like a camper blowing on coals, the wind whipped the fire fronts into more dry timber. The Fan fire flared in the wind, and burned a backcountry cabin near Sportsman Lake. On August 3, at a ranch on the park's northern border, members of the Church Universal Triumphant stood face-to-face with the fire and chanted a rapid incantation. Ed Francis, vice president of the cult, who had threatened to sue the park over the fire, said the prayers "turned the winds" from the ranch. Millions of gallons in water drops helped, too.

Each dry front touched off new small fires that went on the board in the fire cache. Half of the lightning strikes were catching fire. By August 5, there were forty-five.

On August 8, as Henley watched, the Red fire doubled in size and joined with the Shoshone into one big fire, burning around the thumb and the south arms of Yellowstone Lake.

On August 11, a backburn on the North Fork made a major run north, spotting across the Firehole River into a pretty drive-through loop called the Firehole Canyon Drive. The loop was closed to traffic. Dave Poncin, off for a few days, was called to command the North Fork fire. What fire forecasters had predicted for the rest of the summer, happened in just nine days.

On Aug. 15, another dry cold front crossed the park, packing winds of 20–25 mph and gusts to 40 mph. Relative humidity ahead of the fire was 7 percent. The fire leaped into the crowns of young lodgepole pine thought to be firebreak and raced toward Madison Junction, the grassy confluence of the Gibbon and Firehole rivers where in 1870 explorers of the first national park camped. Two years later Yellowstone was created and the mountain behind the spot named National Park Mountain.

At noon the fire was burning extremely hot in the Firehole Canyon, and the wind carried spots across the highway. "It kinda looked like a blowtorch coming over the road," said Poncin.

At 2:00 P.M., flames loomed atop National Park Mountain. The Madison campground was evacuated as burning trees hundreds of feet above threw sparks hundreds of yards across the rivers and touched off fire in the cured grass. It burned west down the Madison River and north along the Gibbon. The fire also leaped the road to West Yellowstone and began climbing over the bluff to the north.

"Not a good day," Poncin wrote that night. "Got our collected butts kicked. A lesson in humility."

Gary Brown, the deliberate and veteran assistant chief ranger, felt for the first time that nature had taken charge.

"I've been in a lot of big-time emergencies, but I've always felt we've been in control. When it jumped the Madison, there wasn't anything we could do about it. That was the first big-time fire. It really blew through there. It was wall-to-wall fire on the rim. Embers like that bounced off us. We were in the wrong place."

The respite was over. "Will They Ever

A torching tree in strong winds. (©Jeff Henry 1988)

dumped on by helicopters. A log kept by the Hamilton Stores gave an example of the vexing traffic problem: August 16—West Yellowstone to Old Faithful closed A.M. to noon. Norris to Madison closed all day. August 17—Madison to Norris open A.M.; closed 1:00 P.M. for balance of day. August 18—Madison to Norris closed. West Gate closed 1:00 P.M. to 4:00 P.M. South Gate closed 7:00 P.M.

Harried rangers complained, said Sholly, their chief:

> Field officers wanted to close down. And here's the superintendent with concessioners and communities and political life, all saying "don't tell anyone this is closed, because I make my whole living from it." And I'm sitting here on operations [deciding] what to do that is safe but still provide for the least political and economic impact. Some staff said we played Russian roulette. I think we did great. Look at the safety record. No one got hurt. We kept open as long as we could.

Brown, the liaison with the local staff, said, "We offered an awful lot of people the opportunity to see an awful lot of fire. Maybe we gained support for our program. The day it came over the rim at Madison, you couldn't find a parking spot."

But the number of tourists dropped precipitously as travel grew difficult. Area businesses that do 90 percent of their business in three months, and make their profit in August and September, saw it blow away with the wind.

On August 20, a helicopter brought George Henley fresh food, and dropped off two radio technicians to work on equipment. His little lookout was filled with batteries and equipment. The chopper left with plans to retrieve the workers in the afternoon. It never came back.

Vertol helicopters dipped from rivers where they could and from Yellowstone Lake. (©Jeff Henry 1988)

Cease?" asked a local headline.

At times, the smoke and fire danger were so high that rangers drove pilot cars to move tourists to their reservations at the Old Faithful Inn or other hotels. The roads were closed one minute and open the next.

Driving through the smoke was unsettling and exhilarating. Tourists could peer through thick smoke and suddenly come upon a fire, small and unattended, or a crown fire being

"The wind increased to 40 to 50 mph in the afternoon, causing all the park's fires to burn violently," Henley wrote in a full-page journal entry. "There was a huge fire at Flagg Ranch. The south entrance road closed. The smoke was very thick. I thought the fire was coming toward me."

The technicians walked down, leaving Henley alone in the smoke. "That was one of the worst days up there," he said later. "I couldn't tell what was happening."

What was happening came to be known as "Black Saturday." By midafternoon, Yellowstone's fires were raging. Huge convection columns rose all over the park as gale-force winds up to 70 mph pushed the huge fire fronts toward the northeast with walls of flame 100 to 300 feet high. Bob Barbee toured the park by helicopter and called it Armageddon.

Grant Village was threatened again as the wind threw ash and embers, and the decision was made to evacuate for the season.

Just outside the park's south entrance, a tree blew over in the wind, knocking power lines down. A spark started a fire that leaped out of control toward Flagg Ranch. A helicopter with a water bucket was dipping from the Snake River at the time and tried to douse the fire in the first few seconds. But it grew too fast. Flagg Ranch was evacuated. In two hours the Huck fire had grown to 4,000 acres.

In the adjacent Grand Teton National Forest, near Jackson, Wyoming, another fire started the same way near the Aspen Ridge Ranch. When park fire crews arrived it was fifteen acres. By 8:30 P.M. it was 2,000 acres.

In Yellowstone the wind pushed the North Fork fire up the Gibbon River and through the Norris Junction. Poncin's crew could do little but catch spots as they began. A historic soldiers' camp and the old museum at Norris were saved as the fire sent up huge columns of smoke. At Norris, the fire split into two fingers, one heading northwest toward Tower, the other burning along the road toward Canyon Village. Along the way, the fire

Skilled helicopter crews made drops on hot spots. (©Ted Wood 1988)

burned through power lines, forcing fire camps onto generators.

But nothing on Black Saturday could hold a candle to the Clover-Mist fire, which drove eleven miles and burned 46,500 acres. The monster fire now covered 171,000 acres and was pushing hard against the Absarokas that separated Yellowstone from the little tourist towns of Silver Gate and Cooke City, Montana.

Throughout the summer, animals continued their casual grazing patterns, moving to new locations and for the most part staying ahead of the fires. (©Jeff Henry 1988)

IT'S AT MY BACK DOOR," SAID DARREL CRABB of the All-Seasons Inn in Cooke City. "People are loading their cars. The fire is three miles away."

Along a narrow strip of development deep in a valley on the northeast corner of Yellowstone, summer residents and shopkeepers felt surrounded by wildfire.

A fire that had been contained since early July on the Custer National Forest had blown ten miles up a canyon in four hours. The Storm Creek fire suddenly threatened to burn into Yellowstone and Cooke City.

But it was the Clover-Mist fire that scared people in Cooke City, and made them mad. They watched at dusk as the fire billowed over Republic Mountain, tossing logs like matchsticks along the rim of Republic, Amphitheater and Thunderer Pass. Those looking up had to tip their heads back, so high was the rim. But at their feet, sparks burned on the decks of their vacation homes.

Why, they asked, hadn't the fires been put out weeks before? "They were trying to talk this fire out," said Lauren Haugen, who owned a Silver Gate general store.

Truck loads of army soldiers were brought into
Mammoth Hot Springs in late September to help
clean up the remaining hot spots of the North Fork
and Clover Mist fires. (©Ted Wood 1988)

As Black Saturday ended, the ridge of mountains held, just as park officials had predicted. But in one awful day, Yellowstone's fires had grown by 157,000 acres, nearly doubling the fire perimeter. The board in the fire cache now listed more than fifty fires. Fire had burned along 100 miles of road in the park. And the weather outlook was bleak: at least another week of hotter weather, lower humidity and winds at 15 to 25 mph. Bushes and smaller trees in the park—the material that carried fire—now contained less than 2 percent moisture.

That night, Henley could see from his lookout windows the flames of the Red fire below Mt. Sheridan. What had once been a couple of smokes was now a mass of fire and smoke that had moved gradually across the bottom of Yellowstone. He could see, too, the Mink fire from the Bridger-Teton Forest, burning actively across Yellowstone Meadows to the southwest, and into the Thorofare, a broad and beautiful wilderness area used heavily by pack trips.

On Sunday, August 21, the army arrived. After nearly a month of fire fighting, many of the 3,500 regular crews on Yellowstone's fires needed a break. Nearly 80 percent of the nation's fire crews were on duty, half of them in Yellowstone. The 1,200 infantrymen from Fort Lewis, Washington, were pushed through a crash course in fire fighting and sent to a new fire camp outside Cooke City near the Crandall Ranger Station of the Shoshone National Forest. Within a day, the camp resembled a war staging area, with heavy smoke, the staccato of helicopters and rows of olive green pup tents lined up with military precision. The young troops stripped off camouflage fatigues and put on the bright yellow fire-resistant shirts, picked up water bottles, helmets, shovels and hoes to practice digging fire lines. They joked about trading M-60 machine guns for Pulaskis and McCleods, and battling bears, rattlesnakes, tics and heat exhaustion.

Larry Boggs, a new incident commander from California, rolled into Cooke City with an order to keep fire out. "People were extremely bitter and felt the park service was lying to them, either real or perceived," he said. Boggs began clearing timber from around the two towns, and holding meetings. On the Shoshone Forest, he brought in bulldozers, for now the fire was on the edge of several drainages leading to timber areas, ranches and summer homes. "We are not going to abandon Cooke City or any other location," said Boggs.

"We're glad you're here," said Dena Archer, who was building a vacation home in the woods.

A day later, another incident commander arrived in Cooke City to fight the Storm Creek fire. Dave Liebersbach of Alaska found that the fire had made a long run and was now just four miles north of Silver Gate. It was nearly inaccessible, with steep, slippery canyons and thick woodland, both in and out of the park. Supplies had to be carried in by pack train.

Meanwhile, in Yellowstone's midsection the North Fork fire had again become a threat to a development. Tourists returning to their cabins at Canyon Village Tuesday night, August 23, found handwritten notes on their doors: "Canyon Lodge is being evacuated by the National Park Service. Please come to the front desk to claim any outstanding balance and turn in your key. Thank you." They could stay until daybreak but many chose not to. By midnight, the entire western horizon appeared to be afire, a rosy orange, ominous glow from a massive backburn set by Poncin's crews a mile from the village. In the still night, the whoosh of each tree igniting traveled for miles. By dawn, when lodge employees knocked on doors, many beds were empty.

"We may be the last of the Mohicans as far as tourists are concerned," said Joe Palat of Pocatello, Idaho. "We've been to Yellowstone before, but not with all this excitement."

The North Fork had virtually cut Yellowstone in half, and the number of tourists

On "Black Saturday,"
August 20, 40–60-mph
winds whipped fires into
a raging inferno. The
charred trees give
witness to the intensity.
(©Ted Wood 1988)

By the third week in August, the North Fork and Clover-Mist fires had practically joined. Smoke plumes from both fires seemed to rim Yellowstone Lake, rising 40,000 feet high. Lake Hotel is visible in the foreground. (©Ted Wood 1988)

dropped even more. TW Services, which operates hotels, cabins and campsites, estimated a $5-million loss. Marketing Vice President John Olson, watching workers board up the lodge and cafeteria at Canyon, mulled in his head advertising slogans for another year: "Yellowstone: You'll Love the Way It Hasn't Changed." By 10:00 A.M., 750 guests and employees were gone. A chalk X marked each door on a cabin known to be empty.

Through the day the sun burned golden red through the smoke. Ashes drifted in windows and fire trucks began taking up positions around the complex.

One-half mile to the south, Steve and Angela Fuller worked to save their home. Steve, a photographer and chief of maintenance at Canyon, had laid sprinklers on his lawn. Fire hoses ran from an old reservoir to soak the house. The trees were cleared of snags. And inside the rustic shingled house, shelves were emptied as the family packed to leave. The home lay directly in the path of one of the fire's fingers headed toward Otter Creek.

By now the North Fork fire had become so long and ungainly that it was split into battlegrounds. Poncin remained at the rear and Kurt Bates was recalled and placed at Canyon, in the face of the fire. There was more than enough work.

Fire line that had held for forty-five days west of Old Faithful suddenly gave way as sparks blew across and started new fires. Crews rushed to set up spike camps. A lost fire there meant trouble again for Old Faithful.

There was concern, too, for the town of West Yellowstone. Poncin's crews used explosives to dig quick fire lines from Seven-Mile Bridge to the park boundary. Fire was burning along the road. On Yellowstone Lake, crews were put in boats to save Trail Creek Cabin in the deep south arm of the lake. And on the Thorofare, flames 200 feet high and 200 yards wide rushed at fire fighters trying to protect the Fish & Game cabin. They hid beneath shelters, then went back to save the cabin.

On the next day, flames roared toward Canyon Village. The horizon turned black in midafternoon. Journalists and tourists huddled in the parking lot with helpless fire fighters. They were safe from the flames but in the way, said Bates. "There could have been people hurt, no doubt. It raised the frustration level with having to contend with people and fire fighters too."

Fire fighters couldn't keep up with the fire. "By the time they'd get hoses off the trucks, they were packing them back in and they were leapfrogging to the front of the fire," said Shaun Stanley, a photographer in the village.

Yet, for all the excitement in Yellowstone, there were greater fire fighting needs elsewhere.

On August 26 a summit meeting was held by the Boise Interagency Fire Center, the agency that decides where the nation's fire fighting resources go.

A million acres were burning in the West. California had five major fires, Idaho had seventeen. Ten were burning elsewhere in Montana, twelve in Oregon, seven in Washington. "It's just been a steady drumbeat, just on and on and on," said Arnold Hartigan of the Boise center.

Yellowstone was asked to give up 1,000 fire fighters, helicopters, and infrared aircraft. That forced a crucial decision in Yellowstone: no longer could crews surround a fire, dig lines, and try to hold it. The fire was racing too fast, spotting, torching and crowning. The usual way of fighting was failing in Yellowstone. Fire bosses decided to withdraw forces to developed areas and defend them.

The park stopped charging its $10 entry fee, but the only people that Yellowstone wanted to attract were fresh fire fighters and helicopter pilots. The U.S. Forest Service agreed to hire 4,000 people off the streets. And Senator Wallop of Wyoming put out a national call for more private helicopters, and asked the Defense Department to send sixty jeeps, twenty buses, satellite-linked telephones and radios. The military also sent an additional 1,200 army troops.

Foaming a National Park Service residence in preparation for an advancing fire. (©Jeff Henry 1988)

Public Relations

LIKE A LOT OF KIDS, GARRETT Robinson saw *Bambi*, with its frightening fire scene, at a theater near his home during the summer of 1988. The difference was that Garrett's home was in Yellowstone National Park.

So when his father asked him to walk in the cool ashes of one of the park's burned areas, Garrett said no.

"Here I was," recalled George Robinson, "the chief naturalist of Yellowstone National Park, with all this scientific training that fire is beneficial, with a son, who, for his entire six years of life has been taught that fire is bad. He's had fire drills at school. His mother and I have told him about getting out of the house in case of fire. There was smoke all summer, and when the fire approached Mammoth, it was scary."

For Yellowstone officials, dealing with the aftermath and attitudes about fire was just as trying as putting the fires out. "You can change someone's mind with facts," Robinson likes to say. "But it's tougher to convince the heart."

Even before the fires were out, the park began an unprecedented public relations campaign to convince the world that Yellowstone was OK. The effort was aimed, in part, at recouping the economic losses in the tourist industry. It also defended the park's natural fire policy.

But the park was in need of philosophic PR, too. For although the landscape was healthy, the ideal was not.

"We've been vilified," said Robinson. "There is a common misconception that Yellowstone has been desecrated. We're not attempting to make black beautiful. Fire has two faces. We need to be mindful of that. It's an unparalleled educational opportunity and challenge."

Superintendent Barbee went to Europe in November 1988 to help convince tour guides that Yellowstone was still a good place to stop. Money from national parks all over America was diverted to Yellowstone to build nature trails in burned areas, erect thirty wayside exhibits, and create both a museum exhibit at Grant Village and a traveling show on fire.

A three-member FIRE committee began traveling through Wyoming, Montana and Idaho doing "fire interpretation and resource education" before clubs and school classes. "Not to apologize or justify, but simply to interpret the fire and what can be expected in the future," said Robinson.

Movies, videos, brochures, games and position papers were churned out for use in the park and for organizations like the Wyoming Travel Commission.

Park officials expected a "Mount St. Helens effect" after the fire. Tourism flourished after the volcano disaster, out of simple, if perhaps, morbid, curiosity. But they were unsure how long that effect would last.

The best public relations was the park itself—"people coming here and actually walking into a burned area and reaching down a few centimeters and seeing flexible roots," said Robinson.

What appealed to Garrett would appeal to anyone.

"We will emphasize that childlike sense of wonder—to look at things with an open heart and see beauty in everything. A significant number of people will come to Yellowstone to see that one remaining tree. And they'll be stunned to see that the charred tree is, in fact, a tree of life."

Park biologists believe fires will create better wildlife habitat than existed before, clearing deadfall on the forest floor, thus allowing grasses and other food to grow. (©Ted Wood 1988)

Green shoots of regrowth near Elk Park in fall 1988. (©Jeff Henry 1988)

IN DEPRESSING SMOKE, VOICES OF DESPAIR rose around the park. The haze had drifted 500 miles to Denver, turning sunsets over the Rockies red. In Jackson, Wyoming, the dark air contained 700 percent the usual particulates and health officials warned elderly, children and people with respiratory problems to curtail outdoor activity.

The T-shirt market boomed, poking fun at Yellowstone's fire policy. A political cartoon offered scorched teddy bears in a fire sale, and called them Barbee Dolls after the besieged superintendent. A sign in West Yellowstone invited people to a Labor Day Barbee-que. Montana Representative Ron Marlenee called for the superintendent's resignation, and Wallop called on Park Director William Penn Mott to resign.

It was clear that Congress would step in and review the summer's fires. Wallop, running for reelection in Wyoming, said his Public Lands Subcommittee would review the handling of the fire. "You can't have a 100-year event and say there's nothing to be looked at. We are going to see fire damage all the rest of our lives."

Wolf Lake fire aftermath.
(©Jeff Henry 1988)

As he spoke, six miles of the old fire lines west of Old Faithful "blew out," and sixty fire fighters were dropped by helicopter to camp by the fire and dig two-foot-wide fire lines in the duff.

The Storm Creek fire also blew up, and burned into a drainage called Lost Creek. Residents of Cooke City and Silver Gate were warned that an evacuation was imminent. Seventy-five fire engines, bulldozers and crews drove into the towns, jostling for parking spots next to the rustic log cabins along the main drag. Throughout the day, residents carried away what they could, deciding what to keep and what to risk. Photographs, antique furniture, and many prize racks of elk were packed to go.

To the west of Cooke City, a new fire called Hellroaring was leaping ahead in quarter-mile steps toward the park. A decision was made to make a bold 20,000-acre backburn to protect Gardiner and Jardine, Montana, and Mammoth Hot Springs.

The North Fork fire also burned inexorably toward Roosevelt-Tower, and on August 30, near Canyon, sent a treetop flame thrower racing two miles along the edge of Hayden Valley. Fire leaped the Yellowstone River. "It's gone," said Bernie Spanogle, a district fire manager directing helpless crews along the river. "It will probably burn to the Clover-Mist fire."

On top of Mt. Sheridan, things got worse for Henley.

"The smoke became almost unbearable," he wrote August 30. "Choppered out." It was an abbreviated message for a harrowing day. Henley could see flames out the window. Wood was stacked against the building and a propane tank sat outside. In the thick smoke, Chief Ranger Sholly flew in to rescue him.

That night, from the Heart Lake cabin, Henley sat outside and looked up at the flames near his lookout and listened for the explosion of the tank. It never came. The next morning, when he returned, the lookout was intact.

"I put out another small fire near the lookout and worked on a few smokes below the heliport," he wrote September 1.

That evening, as the winds calmed in Yellowstone and the night air cooled, a rare "downslope" breeze rushed through the Madison Canyon in a westerly direction, pushing the North Fork fire directly at West Yellowstone. Ash began falling in the streets, where stunned residents stood watching an eerie red glow just beyond the last row of buildings. Fifty fire engines took positions around the little town of 750, and some began hosing the roofs of houses. Firemen passed out an evacuation plan.

The fire came within 1¼ miles of the village and sent up a huge column of smoke lit by the setting sun. "It was enough to scare the hell out of people," said Denny Bungarz, the affable incident commander now in charge of the North Fork fire. A bulldozer line had been dug earlier in the day along the park's boundary, and that night Bungarz's crews set a backburn from the line, adding to the fire show. Explosions periodically shook buildings as fire crews blasted fire lines.

Bungarz assured residents that West Yellowstone was "defensible," but a group of Mormons were not content to leave the work to the professionals.

Clyde Seely, owner of the Three Bears Lodge, called a Mormon brother in Idaho. Through an emergency network in the church, farmers all up and down the Snake River Valley soon were loading pumps, pipe and sprinklers onto semitrailer beds and driving through the night. By 9:00 A.M. Friday, they were laying pipe, and thirty-foot sprinklers were wetting the woods from West Yellowstone's east boundary one-half mile into the trees. "This is making me a hoot happier," said Lee Seely.

As the Labor Day weekend began, there was no holiday air in Yellowstone. Nine thousand fire fighters, including 2,500 federal troops, were making last-ditch stands as the

Mormon farmers in Idaho donated their irrigating equipment and time to help save West Yellowstone. Icicles hang from the trees while the sprinkling continues. (©Jeff Henry 1988)

fire perimeter reached nearly 1 million acres. The daily fire maps made it look like a park ravaged by black cancer, crawling from southwest to northeast.

To make matters worse, a new forecast now predicted another gusty, dry, cold front to blow over Yellowstone by Tuesday or Wednesday. Another 300,000 acres of fire could be added to the fire in three days.

On Saturday, the Mormon farmers laid pipe on the town's south side to prevent a fire now threatening Island Park, Idaho, a few miles away. The same freak wind had blown the North Fork fire back across the very spot where the woodcutter had dropped his cigarette. Officials advised the owners of 225 summer cabins to evacuate.

And Montana's Governor Ted Schwinden declared all of Montana off limits to outdoor recreation, hunting, fishing, boating. Near Old Faithful, Hot Shot crews gave up their efforts to stop fire headed for the famous geyser. They couldn't keep it inside the line in the wind, so they were diverted to saving cabins near Island Park.

On the opposite side of Yellowstone, fire roared like a freight train down Slough Creek toward the Silver Tip Ranch, an exclusive resort. Crews surrounded the buildings while helicopters doused the nearby trees with water. Caught in a narrow valley, the fire whipped into a fire storm, a hurricane of smoke and flame.

Roger Sadler was one of two helicopter pilots dropping water. A former Vietnam chopper pilot with three Purple Hearts and two Distinguished Flying Crosses, Sadler saw the fire storm develop, with 150-foot flames 300 yards across. His wind indicator showed 70 mph. "We were in the eye of the storm," he said. Down below, as the smoke and fire whirled around them, thirty-nine fire fighters hid beneath their fire shelters.

Sadler landed his chopper in a slough to wait for the fire storm to pass. When he took another look, the buildings had been saved and a few trees around them were green — those doused by water. The rest of the narrow valley, he said, was "burned to a crisp."

With the fire now only one wooded ridge away from Silver Gate and Cooke City, and 40-mph winds forecast for midweek, the towns were evacuated Sunday morning, and fire boss Liebersbach took a daring step to protect them.

A huge bulldozer gash, six blades wide and three miles long, was cut Sunday through the woods a half mile west of Silver Gate, from one side of the valley to the other. Six hundred fire fighters lined the gash as helicopters dropped jellied gasoline and ignited 5,000 acres on the west side. Crews stood by long fire hoses in case the fire jumped the line. There was risk that the fire would jump and burn through Silver Gate, but without the burn, the Storm Creek fire would burn it anyway.

By Monday Liebersbach was bluntly giving his crews only a 25-percent chance of keeping fire from overrunning the two towns. "We're in an event here which is going to be fire history. We're going to do everything we can, but I don't think we can hold it. We can't physically save all the structures."

As a sheriff barked evacuation orders through a bullhorn and bulldozers cut dirt circles around both towns, Judy Tucker carried antiques from her Pine Edge Cabins. Jean Hayes, who retired in Silver Gate, packed a trailer with special things. "It makes you feel like you may not see your house again," she said. Mary and Bob Hightower drank one last drink from the deck of their $150,000 log home. "We just put the blinds up," said Hightower. "It's been three years finishing it, and now it could be gone on Monday."

At Cooke City's boundary, someone added a letter to the city name. It now read Cooked City.

At 6:30 P.M. on Tuesday, September 6, the wind picked up in the Soda Butte Valley. Banners whipped, dust and smoke whirled up the

street. An ember from the burnout blew across the bulldozer line and landed in trees behind the Range Rider, a bar and motel at the edge of Silver Gate. A fire truck and crews rushed to catch it, but it got away.

Within minutes fire was in the treetops on the north hill, 200 yards behind a row of cabins. The wind pushed flames into another tree, and another. It raced up the canyon, just outside the dozer lines. Within ten minutes a long, narrow strip of flames had raced the length of Silver Gate and begun burning toward Cooke City, two miles away. A shed caught fire. Crews sprayed other buildings in town.

When the North Fork fire moved uncomfortably close to Old Faithful, the Idaho farmers were brought in to install a sprinkler system as one line of defense. And power poles were wrapped with fire shields to keep them from burning. (©Ted Wood 1988)

**Old Faithful Inn
September 6, the day
before the fire arrived.**
(©Jeff Henry 1988)

On the afternoon of September 7, a fireball headed for the parking lot at Old Faithful. (©Jeff Henry 1988)

Many miles to the south the ill wind blew the Clover-Mist fire twenty miles across the Absaroka Range and down Jones Creek, the valley that Vice President Bush had visited. Like a blowtorch, the fire blackened it from rim to rim, burning 40,000 acres in fourteen hours. So fierce was the fire that it struck down birds in flight. Fire engines were called out from Cody, Wyoming, to Pahaska Tipi, the old hunting lodge of Buffalo Bill. Pahaska and two

nearby lodges were evacuated, and the east gate of Yellowstone closed.

The same wind blew the North Fork fire to within a mile of Old Faithful late Tuesday, and promised to blow through the night. Fire officials knew that the parking lots and sidewalks provided a good defense, but three historic lodges stood at the edge of the geyser, and several stores, a gas station and dozens of rustic cabins were spread in the trees. The

Old Faithful Inn was also full with nearly 600 guests. The park made plans to evacuate in the morning.

On September 7, tour buses rolled up to the big wood doors of the inn, and elderly groups walked on. Most were unaware of the danger building to the west. Other guests who had planned to stay were awakened at 8:00 A.M. with a knock and notice to leave by 10:00 A.M.

By noon the inn was empty, but tourists still milled about the complex, watching Old Faithful and buying ice cream at the Hamilton Store.

"We expect the fire to bump our line," said Denny Bungarz to gathered reporters. "We'll let the fire hit us." The wind picked up enough to push the inn's flag straight east, but Bungarz was unphased. "We could no nothing and it would survive."

The fire, fanned by high winds, suddenly raced down the ridge west of Old Faithful into the developed are. A wall of flame overran some of the guest cabins behind the Hamilton Store, but the store did not burn. (©Ted Wood 1988)

81

B Y 3:00 P.M., FIRE BEGAN SHOWING IN THE crowns of trees to the west of Old Faithful. Aircraft roared low and sprayed long pink veils of retardant on the ridge. The flames smoked, retreated and boiled again. Tall plumes of dark smoke drifted across the sun and cast dark red shadows. Young inn employees sat on their cars in the parking lot, drinking beer and cheering as flames leaped and disappeared.

At about 4:00 P.M., a low roar began in the woods beyond the parking lot. The air turned dry and hot and the color of soot. Park fire crews hauled hoses in the wind to spray on the buildings, but the water blew away short of the shingles. Sparks flew from the hillside and landed on the dry and needle-covered roofs of the old cabins, igniting fires. Two engine crews raced between the rows of cabins to put them out.

Choking tourists, their eyes watering, ran for their cars. RVs pulled out, rocking in the wind. Employees jammed blankets and stereos in their small cars. They no longer were cheering. A ranger screamed at people to drive away. Someone took a frightened clutch of

**Some of these guest
cabins in the Old
Faithful area burned.**
(©Ted Wood 1988)

college students to the seats at Old Faithful, where they waited in the smoke.

Embers the size of fists blew through the parking lot. Firebrands banged on safety helmets. An old garage caught fire, the flames blowing yellow and parallel to the ground. Inside, an oil truck exploded. Boiling gobs of red flame rolled over and through trees. Fire extinguishers hanging on the cabins exploded in the heat as the cabins burned to the ground. Fire trucks raced through the dark.

Sparks landed on the ranger station and were put out. One spark blew onto the tall roof of the inn's right wing. Sprays put it out, and a fire truck began pumping water into a rooftop sprinkling system. Water gushed over the dry shingles like a rainstorm.

On the hill east of Old Faithful, a backdrop to many photographs, a small spot of flame roared to life. It had been thrown there by the wind. As it spread it burned over the hill and out of sight.

The fire storm lasted an hour. No one was hurt, but the event left many shaken. Several Hamilton Store employees broke down and cried. They had been through a forest fire nightmare. Chief Ranger Sholly said later that tourists should not have been in the complex: "We didn't close it down quick enough. Something screwed up somewhere."

Nineteen cabins were burned to the ground. An employee dormitory across the road was damaged along with three storage buildings, a restroom, five vehicles, a water tank and a TV transmitter station. Rick Gale, an area commander, later said that if the 40-mph wind had shifted two or three degrees, the Old Faithful Inn would have burned.

Weeks of felling and trimming trees had paid off. A sprinkler system set up by the Mormon farmers saved a power line. "One of the good things is that it fireproofed the Old Faithful area," said Bungarz.

By dusk the smoke began to lift, and those trapped at Old Faithful were escorted in long convoys through the Firehole River Valley, now burning on both sides.

It had been Yellowstone's worst day.

In Cooke City the winds had blown the fire along the north edge of town and east to Cooke Pass, a small settlement of summer homes. Ten cabins, five sheds and a television transmitter were lost. A swatch of trees on the hillside behind Cooke City was scorched. Both the Storm Creek and Crandall fire camps were evacuated.

The Clover-Mist fire, as feared, roared down the creek drainages from the Absarokas, past ranches and the Crandall Ranger station and toward scenic Sunlight Basin. Five homes, seventeen trailers, three outbuildings, a store, two vehicles and two boats were burned at Crandall, Wyoming. The fire jumped U.S. 212.

And at Canyon Village, stiff winds pushed fire to within three feet of the visitor center. Heroic efforts by engine crews knocked fire down, and no buildings were lost.

One hundred thousand acres burned in Yellowstone on Wednesday, September 7, and for the first time, fires destroyed private property. As fire crews assessed the damages, weather forecasters warned them to brace for more. Another cold front, possibly with moisture, but with 60-mph winds, was expected Saturday.

In Washington, President Reagan was briefed on the fires in the West. More than $270 million had been spent to fight fires that had burned 3.6 million acres—an area larger than Connecticut. Yellowstone's 52 fires now covered 1.2 million acres in and around the

park. More than 30,000 fire fighters from 39 states and 2,500 soldiers had been on the fire lines.

Wyoming's congressional delegation asked that Wyoming be declared a disaster area, and Senators Wallop and Simpson called again for the resignation of National Park Service Director William Penn Mott – "for the simple reason that he continues to find some reason to celebrate this event while all the rest of us are suffering."

At the height of the fire storm, frightened civilians rushed to get away from the Old Faithful Inn as fire fighters prepared its roof for possible fires.
(©Ted Wood 1988)

Crews mop up burned
cabins following the Old
Faithful fire. An area
commander later said
that if the 40-mph wind
had shifted two or three
degrees, the Old Faithful
Inn would have burned.
(©Jeff Henry 1988)

An old storage shack in the Old Faithful parking lot went up in flames when embers set the roof on fire. The communications dish next to it was spared. (©Ted Wood 1988)

Research in the Park

SCIENTISTS LINED UP TEN DEEP AT Yellowstone's gates before the smoke cleared, waiting for Henry Shovic to finish his shovel work.

"Who wants my information?" Shovic asked as he stepped into a burned area. "Hydrologists, geologists, wildlife specialists, those studying grizzlies, elk migration, small mammals, woodpeckers, landslide potential, fire behavior, snowpack. All kinds of studies."

Shovic, a short, serious soil scientist, a man accustomed to quietly digging into processes that take years, found himself one of the most harried men in the park in the autumn of 1988. He had to finish his work between the time the fires went out and snowfall. "All this disappears in the spring. The grass grows. All the ash blows away."

He scraped the end of a tile spade through a layer of gray ash. "It's about five centimeters thick. Moderate heating. But look." He scraped deeper, to gray soil entwined with flexible roots, still alive and ready to grow in the spring. Even though this was a crown fire, with fifty-foot flames, most canopy burns show moderate soil burns. I've heard congressmen say the soil is sterilized. It's the universal opinion of soil scientists that it is not. The ecology is sitting under the ground, just waiting."

Using aerial photographs shot from U2 airplanes and Learjets, Shovic's small army of soil scientists mapped the entire 1 million burned acres—half the park—into categories of intensity. One-tenth of 1 percent of the soil was sterilized, and only 50 percent, or 573,000 acres, was blackened by crown fires. Another 367,000 acres burned on the ground in woodland, and 55,000 acres of meadow and sage burned.

With that baseline data, other scientists can monitor changes in the park in a variety of disciplines. The National Park Service was flooded with hundreds of research proposals for Yellowstone, research that could cost $10 million.

"It's an opportunity to study the effects of a large-magnitude fire on a functioning ecosystem. It probably happens once in a lifetime of any researcher," said Jim Schmitt, a geology professor at Montana State University.

Historically, Congress approves research money after disasters. It took the 1959 earthquake that killed campers outside the park to prompt the first full-scale geologic mapping of Yellowstone. National Park research accounts for less than 5 percent of the park's budget. According to the National Parks and Conservation Association, the Park Service has never asked Congress for a substantial increase in research funds. The fires provided an opportunity to do so.

Park officials say there are more pressing problems, like a $1-billion backlog of maintenance projects, just to keep the national parks from deteriorating.

But Yellowstone's fires revealed a shortcoming of science. "We didn't have enough of it," said John Varley, the park's chief of research. Fire behavior was based on inadequate models. The weather forecasts were wrong. Key decisions were based on limited knowledge. There was nothing in the sixteen years of studying natural fire that prepared the park for 1988.

"We thought we were playing football between the two goal lines. Whereas we were, in the last sixteen years, playing between the two forty-yard lines," said Varley. "I don't know how we could have predicted a fire season that burned 1 million acres with the information available."

By the end of the first week in October, most of the fires were all but out and the air finally cleared over Yellowstone. Aerial views revealed the erratic, or mosaic, pattern in which the fires burned. This view is of the Wolf Lake burn, west of Hayden Valley. (©Ted Wood 1988)

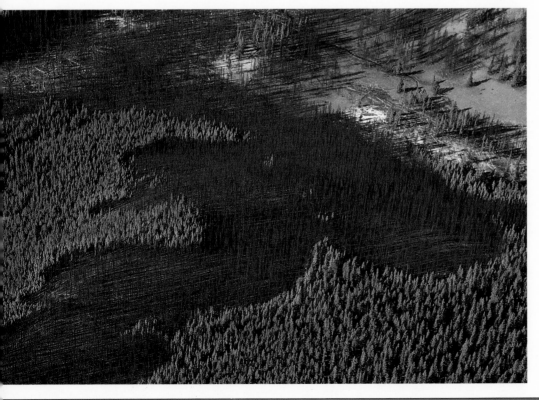

Soil scientists used aerial photographs of the mosaics to map the entire burned area. The maps become part of a baseline data that will be used over the years to study the park in a variety of scientific disciplines. (©Ted Wood 1988)

Mott called "absolutely untrue" the persistent charges that fires weren't being vigorously attacked. "We have been fighting these fires for seven weeks now, using every strategy known . . . but to very limited success."

U.S. Forest Service Chief Dale Robertson said fire fighters were doing the best job they could. "In hindsight, we would have tried to put out every fire . . . that we could have."

Reagan dispatched two of his cabinet officials to tour Yellowstone and other fire areas. Interior Secretary Hodel and Agriculture Secretary Richard Lyng couldn't have picked a worse day.

On the eve of their arrival, Saturday, September 10, the North Fork reached the lip of the mountains overlooking park headquarters at Mammoth. A rolling orange and black line filled the horizon. Park families were put on alert. The lodge was emptied of tourists and opened to fire fighters and journalists.

The fire also sent up a sinister-looking column near Tower-Roosevelt, a rustic collection of cabins around an old lodge scattered among old and beautiful trees. The shingle roofs were covered with tinder-dry moss. Crews set up an irrigation system which raised the humidity level around the lodge. They also foamed the roofs. Fire burned all night around Tower—"Anyone who had not been around fire would have thought that was the end of the world," said Bates—yet his fire fighters saved everything.

At 5:30 A.M. on Saturday, September 10, the cold front roared into Yellowstone. One thousand people were evacuated at Mammoth's headquarters and Yellowstone Lake. The tiny communities of Jardine, Montana, population fifty, and Duck Lake, population thirty, left their homes.

Hodel called the fires a "disaster" and said Yellowstone's fire policy would be changed "so we won't ever face this again. It's obvious no one would have implemented the policy if they had foreseen this kind of year."

As fire burned within a mile of Mammoth Hot Springs, Lyng called the fires "dreadful. I didn't think I'd see anything quite as bad as Mount St. Helens, but I did today."

Superintendent Barbee, his own family evacuated, said the National Park Service had "nothing to apologize for. The myth that this policy is responsible for these fires is insane. The truth is, the best fire fighting effort in the world can't break the back of the fire."

When would it end?

George Henley was the first to know.

"Rain fell for an hour beginning 2:00 A.M.," he wrote in his journal. "Rain and hail. Turned cold." Snow began falling on higher elevations. There was more the next day.

"The station was fogged in all day and snow started falling about 8:00 and continued most of the day. 19 degrees," Henley wrote.

Just as the fire and the rhetoric had reached their horrific peak, Mother Nature stopped it. Three inches of wet snow fell over the weekend.

Fires continued to burn and smoke over hundreds of thousands of acres. The fire map now looked like a single large fire, spread in blobs and fingers over the great park. As the snow melted and dry weather returned, Sholly said, "The fire season is not over. This is a sleeping giant."

The Pentagon sent 1,200 marines. Near Mammoth, crews cut and hauled away sagebrush, installed a sprinkler around the housing area, and wet down short grass along the road to Gardiner, Montana.

The Clover-Mist still burned within its perimeter and helicopters dropped buckets of water daily. Crews on the North Fork fire still built line. They were finally making headway. The Storm Creek fire burned actively near Elk Tongue Creek as it entered Slough Creek. On the Snake River complex, the drudge work of mop up continued, the turning over of stumps and logs, the putting out of every last smoke.

Still camped out, the crews awoke many mornings to frost and huddled around gas

North Fork fire approaching Mammoth Hot Springs, September 10. (©Jeff Henry 1988)

By October, some spot fires were still burning, but the main body of the North Fork fire was out. Fierce winds blew the fire through the forests, leaving expanses of untouched trees. (©Ted Wood 1988)

heaters. Snow and drizzle fell many days.

"Staying warm is becoming difficult," Henley wrote September 13. "Counted twenty small fires south of Heart Lake."

On September 16, Democratic presidential candidate Michael Dukakis stood in the ashes near the Firehole Drive and brought Yellowstone back into the news. But the days of crisis were over. Every day crews gained the upper hand on another fire. Thoughts turned to the future.

"Yellowstone Begins Rebirth," read the headline in the *Washington Post*. News of a few shoots of grass, a sticky geranium and a fireweed in the ash near Grant Village spread like wildfire through the park. Photographers,

no longer able to shoot huge flames, focused on buffalo and elk in the burned timber. And everywhere lodgepole seeds by the millions dotted the ash.

As the smoke lifted and roads opened under sunny, Indian Summer skies, it became apparent that not all the park had burned. Vast areas were spared.

Hundreds of fire crews turned from making fire lines to covering them up, raking the duff of the forest floor back to the original contour. One thousand miles of fire lines had been dug.

Hundreds of fallen tree trunks lay on trails. Overhead, often by a thread of bark, snags hung, threatening hikers. Crews with chain saws were dispatched to clear them before snowfall.

Young elk in burned
area near Madison.
(©Jeff Henry 1988)

"Walked down trail with ax. Cleared trail, mostly burned trees," Henley wrote October 9.

Helicopters continued to shatter the morning quiet of the park, but they now were picking up miles of hose and tons of trash left by fire camps in the backcountry. "We will try to erase the appearance that man was there," said Stu Coleman, in charge of rehabilitation. Bears, weaned from human food years before, had found the camps and were rummaging through the leftovers.

Along the road where sawed tree stumps were an ugly reminder of the fire fight, the public was invited to cut firewood. A logging contractor hauled more out.

Bridges were replaced, pink slurry was washed from buildings. Winter wheat was sown in the thirty-two miles of bulldozer line.

93

Help

WHEN YELLOWSTONE BURNED, Cindy Kessler and the Loyal Order of the Moose had the same urge.

Cindy, eight, went door-to-door collecting money on her street in Chesterfield, Missouri. She taped the coins to a large poster, added hearts and signatures in crayon, and mailed the $3.24 to the fire fighters.

In Washington, D.C., the Moose fraternity made a pledge to raise $1 million for Yellowstone.

From the big and small, Yellowstone received an outpouring of love, money and offers to help. Trees were a common offer, followed by money to feed "starving animals." A family in Maryland mailed pine cones. Children in Albuquerque, New Mexico, offered to send a bale of hay.

The park was touched but could not use every gift.

While some planting was done as landscaping around developed areas, the Park Service wants the burned areas to regenerate by themselves, using the seeds naturally spread by lodgepole pine and resprouted from rhizomes and roots.

And feeding animals goes against natural regulation, the policy in which the animal numbers rise or fall based on severity of winter.

Money donated to Yellowstone will be used for repairing trails, creating fire naturalist displays and scientific research. Children's donations will build a special children's trail in their honor. The trail will go through burned areas and meadows and woodlands skipped by the fires.

George Robinson, the chief naturalist, believes that the offers of trees are based on an image of what Yellowstone should look like, and the mistaken impression that the entire park was burned. "We need a more distant view of Yellowstone," he said. "The one unchanging element of Yellowstone is change." But the reaction of Cindy, the Moose and other people indicated that Yellowstone's pursuit of natural regulation may not have been widely embraced or understood.

Despite a growing acknowledgment that nature is best left alone, there was so much fire in Yellowstone that what should have been an environmental triumph became a political disaster.

Yellowstone, the ecosystem, survived well. Visitors would see how fire created new and interesting patterns and how beneficial fire could be.

But the Summer of Fire set back the cause of natural regulation. Fewer, and smaller, fires would burn. And fire would be viewed more as a tool of man than of nature.

Offers of money and food to help the "starving animals" at Yellowstone poured in from around the country. The decision was made by the park, on the recommendation of outside wildlife experts, not to feed the animals in the winter of 1988–89, but rather to let them forage as usual. Large areas of grass were left unburned, and it was felt that natural systems of population control should be allowed to proceed as usual. (©Jeff Henry 1988)

Steve Fuller, Afterward

IN A MOONSCAPE OF BLACK LIT WHITE by the moon, the skeletons of tree trunks cast a devil's picket fence. A horse and rider slipped across the ash. It was surprising that there was shadow at all.

Steve Fuller, ahead on his horse Ishewa, walked down a steep path they knew by heart. But it was not familiar ground. The Yellowstone woodland had been transformed.

"It is a simple landscape," said Fuller. "It used to be fairly spooky in here."

The moon, now full, pried deep. He rode in silence at the end of a long day of introspection.

Many who love Yellowstone were drawn back to a favorite place after the fire to see the changes. For Fuller, that meant game trails in the backcountry, familiar meadows where his family had played. He was apprehensive. Seared by a summer of fire, he could not view the park the way it looked in autumn light, a place, almost, of benign grace. There were too many memories of walls of flame.

"I always liked the idea of wild Yellowstone at the edge of my house," said Fuller. "I'm all for wildfires. But on that last day, everything was posed for total destruction."

For fifteen years Fuller and his family had lived in a shake cabin near Canyon Village. Angela ran the lodge and Steve shoveled snow from the roofs. In the summer of 1988 he poured water on them. As he rode across Cascade Creek, the memory returned of helicopter water drops in heavy smoke, and ground crews frantically digging line. He crossed a black ridge. "I hated to see this go. I heard it at my house."

An elk bugled in the wind. A snag fell with a crack like a rifle. "I feel like a stranger going into new territory. I don't know this land. It's going to be very interesting in the winter, aesthetically. But that sounds clinical and cold. Mostly I'm awash in emotions."

Yellowstone after fire is both familiar and different. The attractions remain, if scorched at the edges. Fire burned everywhere, but not every place—as if a wild artist splashed gobs of black ink on a green canvas, and edged each splash with a ring of brown.

"This is a bit of a pity," said Fuller, riding into a finger meadow. "We used to call this black bear meadow. There used to be a stump that looked exactly like a black bear. It's gone now."

His horse kicked up ash, which whirled away. The wind through the stumps was low and threatening. "It doesn't even sound like Yellowstone."

The smell of ash brought back memories of the Fullers at home, eyes rimmed with red, with fire in sight. Their home was saved by the grace of God. "I'd like not to live through those weeks again," he said. "Fire is the antithesis of life. It's the other pole, which we deny. It's coming face to face with the facts of mortal existence."

He rode through a meadow cut by a stream, still green, and a favorite lunch spot for the Fullers. "I used to think of two parks: summerscape and winterscape. Now there's a firescape. It's extensive and distinctive enough to classify as a third Yellowstone. And it will be with us for the rest of our lives."

Steve Fuller, longtime resident of Canyon Village, rigged up a sprinkler system to protect his home, all controlled from this fire hydrant. (©Ted Wood 1988)

As THE ASHES COOLED, RESEARCHERS fanned out across the park, still wearing the yellow and green fire-resistant clothes and helmets, to count dead animals and acres burned. Overhead, U2 spy planes and Learjets flew to photograph it foot by foot. Soil scientists and biologists scoured the park.

About .1 percent of the soil had been sterilized, heated to such a degree that rhizomes and grass seeds could not resprout. In nearly all the fire area, life remained below the ash, waiting for moisture and the warmth of the spring sun.

One black bear was burned, and the carcasses of 243 elk, 4 deer, 2 moose and 5 bison were found inside the park. Another 67 elk, 7 moose, 28 deer, and 3 black bears were found dead outside the park. Based on tracking collars of 150 moose, elk, grizzly bears and mountain lions, animals largely moved about as the fires raged, and resumed grazing. Small mammals were killed by the score, and the homes of many were exposed. In the autumn days after the fires, raptors had a field day.

Elk rest in a field that
would become part of
their winter range.
(©Ted Wood 1988)

A panel of scientists recommended that the park not feed any animals during the winter. With the elk population at an all-time high of 30,000, and 34 percent of the winter range burned, many animals were expected to migrate from the park or die during the winter. In the spring, however, expanded grasslands would stimulate another spurt in elk and bison herds.

Slurry killed a few hundred fish in accidental drops in streams. And the fish were stressed by low water levels.

By October, tourists were back in Yellowstone in record numbers. Most were surprised by what they saw. At Gibbons Falls, where the North Fork fire raced through the picnic ground, Ray Helstand of Celina, Texas, stood taking a video.

"I'm shocked there isn't more damage. From what we saw in the paper I expected to come up here and see it just blackened. I read in the Dallas paper that they're going to start a new public relations campaign, and I'll be a big supporter. We'll stay another night. We've had people say they'll never come here. But I'll tell the people back home, 'Hey, it's not as bad as you think.' I just hope people don't stay away from the park because of this—because it's still beautiful."

They stopped fighting fire in Yellowstone on October 17. Thirteen Hot Shots from Wyoming, Oregon and New Mexico rolled up their fire hoses along Elk Tongue Creek and declared the fire line cold. Fires still burned, but they were within safe lines. The fires that had ravaged the park since June were contained.

It had been the single biggest fire-fighting effort in U.S. history. The cost was more than $120 million. One fire fighter, Ed Hutton, died in October when a tree fell on him during mop up on the Clover-Mist fire in Wyoming.

In a preelection push, three congressional hearings were held on the fire. A series of fire reviews also began.

The federal review teams concluded that fire personnel in Yellowstone and the surrounding national forests underestimated the severity of drought conditions, and that the number and size of fires that burned across the park could have been reduced. They recommended that Yellowstone's fire policy be overhauled to take into account weather conditions, the availability of fire-fighting resources and the potential impact on neighboring communities. The furor ensured that Yellowstone would put out fires sooner in the future.

On October 24, George Henley was released from duty on the fire tower. A helicopter arrived to pack him to Mammoth, where he would work another month helping to repair equipment, sharpen shovels, and get ready for the 1989 fire season.

"I finished packing and moved everything to the heliport," he wrote in his last journal entry. "Helicopter 1 came up about 11:00 and I left with it for the season. The door shutter was mostly chewed up by marmots over the last several seasons so I left it uninstalled."

On November 10, snow began falling

steadily in Yellowstone, and within four days had covered up the last smoldering logs. The park closed to traffic and George Henley, the lookout, left for Mexico, and winter in another warm place.

In fall 1988 tourists were back in Yellowstone in record numbers. Most were surprised at how little damage they saw. Others took trips into the wilderness areas to get a firsthand look at the damage. Overall, people were pleasantly surprised. (©Ted Wood 1988)

As winter snuffed out the last of Yellowstone's fires, the world waited with hope for what spring would bring. (©Ted Wood 1988)